MOM, I'M PREGNANT

"In thirty years of dealing with pregnant girls, their boyfriends, their parents, and other young people, I wanted, no, I desperately needed this book. So did others—clergymen, judges and lawyers, social workers, anyone and everyone who must deal, however peripherally, with the unwanted pregnancy of an unwed girl. Perhaps *Mom, I'm Pregnant* couldn't have been written all those years ago. It can now be written and has been, sensitively, wisely, and thoroughly."

> The Reverend Edd Payne
> The Church of Saint Mary
>   the Virgin
> Chappaqua, New York

"*Mom, I'm Pregnant* really does it! This book is helpful to *everyone* concerned—the teenager facing this all too common yet complicated dilemma, her partner, and her parents. Using personal stories to highlight the rich and illuminating educational material, the authors make a presentation which is comprehensive, empathetic, and above all, useful. *Mom, I'm Pregnant* brings clarity where there is usually confusion, presents options where there was thought to be none, and provides warmth and understanding where there was only desperate loneliness. Just when everything seems to be hopeless, this book offers hope."

Dr. Leah C. Schaefer, Ed.D.
The Society for the Scientific
Study of Sex

"*Mom, I'm Pregnant* should become a classic for pregnant teens, their boyfriends, and parents, who are bewildered by the drastic and unexpected consequences of human biology, psychology, and sociology. I would go even further and suggest that it be required reading for all teenagers whether or not they are sexually active, parents who endeavor to understand and love their children, and anyone who desires deeper insight into human sexuality. The book should be acquired by every school and public library in the country, and should be required reading in every course in family life."

Harvey Caplan, M.D.
American Society of Sex
Educators, Counselors and Therapists

1993

MOM, I'M PREGNANT

Sex and teenagers. Up to half of America's teenagers have sex between the ages of 13 and 19.
For a girl, the average age of the first sexual encounter is 16. By the age of 18, two out of three
girls have "gone all the way." The outcome of
such early sexual activity is often pregnancy. It
happens to over one million teenage girls every
year.

Mom, I'm Pregnant is a personal guide for teenagers who are faced with the possibility of
pregnancy — and for parents who care.

"I hope, *Mom, I'm Pregnant* will be widely acclaimed! It analyzes all aspects of legal, emotional, social, financial, and physical problems facing a pregnant teenager. It is refreshingly unbiased about what that decision should be and speaks candidly to the reader about the consequences of each option. Its sensible approach to birth control firmly reminds readers that sexual activity is linked with responsibility and not to be taken lightly. Having *Mom, I'm Pregnant* readily available in community and school libraries may even have a positive effect in preventing unwanted pregnancies."

Ann Parks
Parents Without Partners

"*Mom, I'm Pregnant* offers empathy, direction, and hope in the future. Ms. Witt and Ms. Michael have skillfully produced a down-to-earth, comprehensive and very sensitive personal guide that *all* teenagers should read whether or not they are pregnant. As a parent, I recommend this book for parents who want to develop or improve communication with their teenagers on the subject of sex and pregnancy. We need to be supportive if it should ever happen to . . ."

Maria Vizcarrondo-DeSoto
Young Women's Christian
Association
(Y.W.C.A.)

"*Mom, I'm Pregnant* is an excellent book for adolescent women. First, it is realistic in its presentation of the issues surrounding an unplanned pregnancy and comprehensive in its coverage of the alternatives and their possible consequences. Secondly, the text dispels many of the myths about conception, contraception, pregnancy, and parenthood in a very straightforward matter-of-fact manner. Finally, the book is reassuring. The approach taken by the authors provides the reader the empathy needed while encouraging responsibility for the decisions that must be made and maintained."

Kay Gudmestad
Girls Club of America

"*Mom, I'm Pregnant* is a realistic, objective guide for teenagers facing a decision of what to do once they are pregnant."

Dr. Sol Gordon
Institute for Family Research
and Education,
Syracuse University

MOM, I'M PREGNANT

Reni L. Witt
and
Jeannine Masterson Michael, M.S.W., C.S.W.

A SCARBOROUGH BOOK
STEIN AND DAY/Publishers/New York

First published in 1982
Copyright © 1982 by Reni L. Witt and Larimi Communications
All rights reserved
Designed by Judith E. Dalzell
Printed in the United States of America
STEIN AND DAY/ *Publishers*
Scarborough House
Briarcliff Manor, N.Y. 10510

Library of Congress Cataloging in Publication Data

Witt, Reni L., 1953-
  Mom, I'm pregnant.

  Bibliography: p.
  Includes index.
  Summary: Discusses the emotional and physical consequences of an
unexpected and unwanted pregnancy, and explores the range of decisions
a pregnant girl can make, from abortion to marriage to adoption to
keeping the baby.
  1. Pregnant schoolgirls.   2. Adolescent mothers.   [1. Pregnancy.
2. Unmarried mothers]   I. Michael, Jeannine Masterson, 1928-
II. Title.
HQ759.4.W57   1982   613.9   82-40009
ISBN 0-8128-2874-7
ISBN 0-8128-6173-6 (pbk.)

Acknowledgments

Our deep appreciation to Michael M. Smith, who believed in this project from its inception and without whom this book would not have been written. His support and guidance throughout its writing have been invaluable.

We would also like to express our sincere appreciation to Sol Stein and Patricia Day who had the courage and foresight to publish this book about teenage sexuality and pregnancy during a time of great need and intense controversy. Patricia Day was also our editor and we valued her encouragement and literary guidance. Thanks also to Liz Kelly, assistant editor, for her caring review of our manuscript.

Our book is based on the experiences of thousands of teenage girls who came, over the years, from across the country and Canada to Eastern Women's Center in New York City. We are most grateful to its director, Barbara Methvin, for allowing us to use this facility as well as the assistance of its counseling and reception staff.

Our heartfelt thanks are extended to the young women who shared their hurts and hopes with us during a difficult period in their lives—to the many who answered our questionnaire, and to those who were interviewed and quoted in this book. Names have been changed to protect their privacy.

Many professional people gave generously of their time and knowledge to provide much of the information found within these covers. We would like to thank Kirk Young, M.D., for his medical expertise. Our thanks also to Mrs. Helen Tu of the Edwin Gould Services, and Brian Baker of the Human Resources Administration for their assistance in the areas of adoption and foster care.

We'd also like to thank Ms. Amy Frey of the K.D. McCormick Library at Planned Parenthood-World Population Office in Manhattan. She knows this library like the back of her hand, and seemed to have at her fingertips the books, articles, and papers needed for our research. In addition, we appreciate the kind help of Mrs. Major Lloyd Scott of the Salvation Army who opened their library to us and provided us with many useful publications.

Our thanks are also extended to Renata Karlin Warshaw of Planned Parenthood Federation of America, Hilda Stone of Family Service Association of America, Ann Ulmschneider of National Alliance for Optional Parenthood, Kelly A. Brogan of Future Homemakers of America, Ann Parks of Parents Without Partners, Beverly Richardson of the Grady Memorial Hospital in Atlanta, Georgia, and Edie Moore of the Society of Adolescent Medicine in Granada Hills, California, as well as the Child Welfare League of America, the Alan Guttmacher Institute, the March of Dimes, the International Childbirth Education Association, and the Office of Adolescent Pregnancy Programs of the U.S. Department of Health and Human Services, for providing us with much valuable information.

Many thanks also to Karen Devoti for her secretarial assistance, Bob Del Pazzo for the numerous phone calls he made in our behalf, and K. C. Wilson for his accurate and speedy transcription of our interview tapes.

Statistics found in this book are based on "Adolescent Pregnancy and Childbearing—Rates, Trends, and Research Findings," October, 1981, published by the Department of Health, Education and Welfare with Social and Behavioral Sciences Branch, Center for Population Research, and National Institution of Child Health and Human Development; "Teenage Pregnancy—The Problem That Hasn't Gone Away," 1981, and "11 Million Teenagers— What Can Be Done About the Epidemic of Adolescent Pregnancy in the U.S.," 1976, both published by the Alan Guttmacher Institute-Research and Development Division of Planned Parenthood Federation of America, Inc.; and "Healthy Babies: Chance or

Choice?" published by the March of Dimes Birth Defects Foundation.

The list of clinics and agencies was provided by Planned Parenthood Federation of America, Inc., Family Service Association of America, Society of Adolescent Medicine, Florence Crittenton Division of the Child Welfare League of America, The Salvation Army Maternity Residence and Hospital Facilities, National Abortion Federation, and Y.W.C.A.

Reni L. Witt
Jeannine Masterson Michael
June 1982, New York City

On a personal note, I'd like to thank my husband, Jeffrey W. Kriz, who became a writer's widower a month after our marriage, when I began work on this project. He supported and encouraged me throughout our newlywed months, keeping many special weekend dinners warm, while I wrote and rewrote well into the night. He somehow succeeded in keeping the candles lit without ever blowing out the flames.

—R.L.W.

Loving thanks to my three teenage sons, David, Matthew, and Gregory, who shared my enthusiasm for this project and read early drafts of the manuscript. Their comments about boys' attitudes and feelings were integrated into the sections dealing with male sexuality.

—J.M.M.

Contents

ONE

YOU'RE NOT ALONE

When I first realized I might be pregnant, I felt incredibly happy. I was so proud of my body because it could make a baby. I've always loved children and now I was going to have a baby of my own to dress up, and to care for and to love.—Shana, 17.

I was scared to death when my period didn't start on time. When I told my boyfriend I might be pregnant, he said he didn't want anything more to do with me. I was too ashamed to tell my parents. I didn't know what to do or where to go. I have never felt so totally alone.— Janice, 16.

I was so excited when I learned I was pregnant. I've always wanted a baby. But as the weeks went by, I began to freak out because I'm not ready to be a mother.—Sue, 15.

You're Not Alone

You're not alone. Every year, more than a million teenage girls become pregnant. That's almost two out of every twenty high school girls. As a teenage girl, your chances of becoming pregnant are very high. In fact, most girls who have intercourse will get pregnant before they graduate.

According to the latest figures available, in 1978 there were approximately 1,142,000 pregnancies among teenagers in America. The overwhelming majority were unmarried at the time of conception. A few young women went on to marry before they gave birth, but many more decided to have their babies alone without being married. Nine out of ten girls who gave birth kept their babies. A great number of teenagers felt that abortion was the right choice for them. They made up over 38 percent of teenage pregnancies. Finally, a small percentage of young women had miscarriages.

Dealing with the Facts

How do you fit in with the statistics? The figures show that you are not alone, yet you are not a number. You are a unique person, a special person, with complicated feelings and emotions, with changing relationships, with a developing body, and with a growing understanding about who you are. Because you are a unique person, you will handle the possibility of pregnancy in your own way.

But what is the best way for you? By reading the rest of this book, you will learn how other young women your age handled being pregnant. They share their thoughts and experiences. You'll probably recognize some of your own feelings. Perhaps one of their decisions will seem right for you.

You will also find out about what is happening to your body if you are pregnant. If you decide to keep your baby, you'll learn how to care for yourself and your unborn child. You'll also discover some alternatives to keeping your baby and raising it yourself. If you need to know where to go, that information is also available here. Should you be thinking about having an abortion, you will read about other teenagers' experiences and what is involved for you.

By gathering as much information as you can and by understanding your own needs and feelings, you will learn how to make the right decision for you. After all, learning about yourself is something you will be doing all your life. However, the years between twelve and twenty are especially important in establishing who you are and what your future will be. This is no easy task. Adults often say, "These are the best years of your life." But the teenage years can be very difficult.

For example, school may seem irrelevant. Parents may not seem to understand you. Girlfriends can be competitive. Boys are impossible to figure out. Your body is changing. Sexual feelings are difficult to deal with.

And now, suddenly, you think you might be pregnant. You don't feel like yourself at all. You may feel tired all the time, or sick, or just not right. Your breasts enlarge and become tender. You might be gaining weight. Even early in a pregnancy, you may notice that your waist is thickening. Your jeans don't zip up anymore. Your last period may not have been normal, or you may have skipped your period altogether.

"This Can't Be Happening to Me"

Even if a part of you is happy about the possibility of being pregnant, most girls are worried and concerned about the changes that are happening to them. You might be confused and feeling terribly alone.

Adrienne was 18 and completing her first year at college when she became pregnant.

> *Last semester I got pregnant. I would sit on my bed at night and say, "I don't believe this. This can't be happening to me." I felt numb. My finals were coming up and I couldn't study. I felt paralyzed. I knew I had to do something, but I didn't know what. It was like my life had just stopped.*

Mavis, a high school sophomore, felt just as alone when she became pregnant.

> *I was so afraid to tell my parents. I wished so hard that it would go away. I stopped eating. I drank a bottle of vinegar because I heard that would start your period. But it just made me sick. Then in a soap opera I watched, one of the people had a miscarriage when she fell down some stairs. So I tried that. Nothing worked. It was a nightmare, until I finally went to a doctor.*

3

If you feel that you are the first person ever to have this problem, you're not. Many, many teenagers and even adult women share the same fears and anxieties when faced with an unwanted and unexpected pregnancy. During adolescence, however, these feelings are intensified, especially if you have no one to confide in. Most teenagers, such as Becky, 17, report that the early weeks of pregnancy were the worst time of all.

> *High school graduation was only two months away when I got pregnant. I had been making it with my boyfriend for a couple of months. I knew I'd get caught sooner or later. I just hoped it would be later. When my period didn't come, I was too scared to tell anybody. I didn't tell my boyfriend because I was afraid he'd drop me. I was too embarrassed to tell a teacher or one of the counselors. They'd probably give me a lecture anyway. And I just couldn't tell my parents. I knew what their reaction would be. So for weeks, I lived in panic, praying my period would come. The worst part was pretending that everything was cool. But I was dying inside. I felt so alone. I had no one to turn to.*

Becky finally telephoned a teenage hotline number. The person she talked to gave her the phone number of a nearby clinic and a counselor who was then able to help her.

If you feel as isolated and alone as Becky felt, it may help to know that millions of girls throughout the years have experienced these same feelings. At this very moment across America, thousands of young women your age are going through the same confusion, anxiety, and worry.

However, as troubled as you may feel, it's important to break away from the fear that stops you from getting the help you need. Too many girls wait for several months before taking action.

Angelica, 15, is not alone in her experience with an unplanned pregnancy.

I couldn't believe I was pregnant, even though I had all the signs. I missed my period, I had morning sickness, and I was gaining weight. Still, I was so afraid to tell my mother. So I didn't do anything for months. Finally, my mother figured out I was pregnant. She just asked me point blank, "Are you pregnant?" She was very matter-of-fact about it, like I was this problem she had to solve. We never even talked about it. She just took me to a clinic. The doctor said it was much too late for me to have an abortion. I was over six months pregnant. Now I have to have the baby. I don't really want to have a baby and I'm awfully afraid of labor pains, but now I don't have a choice.

If you think you may be pregnant, it is extremely important to get a pregnancy test as soon as possible. Your parents don't have to know you are getting the test. Chapter 3 contains a section about this simple test for pregnancy—what it is and how you can get one.

The test may show you are not pregnant. But if you are indeed pregnant, early knowledge of that fact will allow you more time to make a decision about the outcome of your pregnancy and carry it out.

If It *Is* Happening

Even though you may feel trapped, you are not. There are many choices to make. Let's take a look at the options.

- You can marry the boy who got you pregnant.
- You can keep your child and raise it yourself.
- You can give your baby up for adoption. There are many loving families who might be right for your baby.
- You can have the baby and release your child to foster parents until you are old enough or better equipped to care for it.
- You can have a legal, medically supervised abortion.

There is no one right or wrong answer, only the one that seems like the best one for you—and your child, should you decide to keep it.

Though not all of these options may be open to you in your unique circumstances, if you are pregnant, you will have to make a decision. Don't let time or circumstances make one for you. The decision will not be easy. In fact, it will probably be the most difficult and important decision you've had to make in your life. Your future may be shaped by the choices you make in the next few weeks and months.

Remember, if you are pregnant, time becomes very important. You have less than three months from the time of your last normal period to make a decision about a first trimester abortion. (A trimester is a time period of three months. The nine months of pregnancy are divided into three trimesters.) If you wait longer than three months, you may still be able to have a second trimester abortion, but it is a more complicated procedure. Should you decide to keep your baby, you have only nine months to prepare for its birth.

So, whether you want to continue your pregnancy or not, there is a great deal to do. Every day counts.

Your Feelings About a Possible Pregnancy

Most girls are in a state of shock when they learn they are pregnant. You've probably said to yourself, "I just don't believe it." You might be extremely upset.

On the other hand, you might be pleased that you are pregnant, even happy about the news. Bette, a high school junior, felt quite joyful when the pregnancy test turned out positive.

> *It was so wonderful to think that I was going to have a baby. I just know I'll make a terrific mother. I'm going to love my baby and dress it in nice clothes. It's going to be so nice to have someone to love and love me back.*

6

Another feeling that many young women have is one of anger. If you feel like screaming or hitting somebody, you're not alone. One high school senior, Kathy, became very angry with her boyfriend.

> *He kept telling me nothing would happen, that*
> *he knew all about those things. And I believed*
> *him! Boy, that was dumb. What makes me so*
> *mad is that he gets away free. I'm the one who*
> *has to go through all the agony. God, it gets me*
> *mad.*

All these feelings are normal. Your emotions might alternate among feelings of joy, anger, and fear. This, too, is completely normal and to be expected. Pregnancy brings enormous change in your body, in your hormones, and in your emotions.

Yet at this time, when your feelings are in a turmoil and you can barely think, you are faced with making an enormous decision about your life, your future, and the future of your baby, should you decide to keep it.

Certainly, the circumstances for making this decision are far from ideal. You may feel totally alone and too inexperienced in life to make a choice that is so vital to your future. On top of all that, you might be feeling physically sick and very tired.

Many girls believe that unwanted pregnancy is a situation they can't master—that this is an adult's problem, not a problem for someone their age. They genuinely don't know what to do. The problem seems overwhelming.

It is important to understand the reasons that can keep many girls, including you, from seeking the help they need.

Some girls wait until it is too late because they *don't want to admit* to themselves that they are pregnant. This may be because they feel ashamed about being sexually active and pregnancy tells the world that they are. In spite of the "new morality," you might still feel deep inside that sex is bad, and, therefore, you are bad. In addition, if you have had sex, you may feel embarrassed at making public such a private, intimate part of your life. Read Chapter 2 in order to learn more about sexual feelings and how they connect with your thoughts and feelings about a possible pregnancy.

7

Another reason many girls delay getting help is that they *don't want a lecture.* Some adults don't know how to respond to a teenager who becomes pregnant. Other people, especially those who care about you, may first react with shock or anger. In Chapter 4, you'll find out how to cope with a "lecture" and how to talk to your parents, should you decide to tell them.

Some teenagers postpone getting a pregnancy test because they are *afraid it will hurt* or that the pelvic examination will be embarrassing. Relax. The urine pregnancy test does not hurt at all. The gynecological exam can sometimes be a little uncomfortable, but a good health care specialist will help to put you at ease. Read Chapter 3 to learn more about the procedure and what it means to you.

Still another stumbling block is *finding a clinic or a doctor.* You've probably never had the experience of going to a clinic or a doctor all by yourself. The back of this book contains a state-by-state list of where to go for assistance. Telephone numbers are provided. It's important to make that phone call soon.

If you are *worried about costs* and where to get enough money, each chapter, starting with Chapter 6, discusses fees and how you can pay for any alternative you may choose.

Another reason for putting off getting help for an unplanned pregnancy is *what having a baby may mean to you.* The dream of having a baby for a teenager is based on the thinking: If you have a baby, you become a mother, and therefore, an adult. More importantly, having a baby means having someone to love and to call your own. But a baby is not a dream. It is a real, living human being with needs of its own. If you are thinking of motherhood, read Chapter 10. Begin planning for your baby realistically.

Some girls hope that the pregnancy will *improve the relationship with a boyfriend.* A teenager may think that a baby will bind her boyfriend to her, or that he will marry her once he knows she is pregnant. Some young men may suggest marriage out of a sense of duty. Many, though, will feel trapped, unprepared for marriage or fatherhood. Yet if you have a close and steady relationship with your boyfriend, marriage might be an option. Chapter 7 can give you some guidelines before making this decision.

On the other hand, a teenage girl may delay seeking help because she fears *her boyfriend will leave her* once the pregnancy is confirmed or that he will insist she have an abortion. This is a real possibility, but one that must be faced. The section in Chapter 4, "Telling Your Boyfriend," may help you to better understand the changes that can occur in your relationship.

A common reason for wanting a baby is *the problems some girls have at home.* They often feel emotionally deprived or that they don't have a good relationship with their parents. These young women want to give their babies what they feel they never received themselves. They want to prove that they will be better mothers than their own mothers have been. This may, unfortunately, be hard to achieve. Becoming a mother is never easy for anybody. It is, in fact, a very difficult choice. Chapter 10 can tell you more about the responsibility of raising a baby.

To some people, *having a baby is a status symbol,* a rite of passage into adulthood. Marriage may not be a consideration. The father of the baby is not expected to help raise the child. Instead, the young woman may assume her own mother and/or extended family will help her care for the baby. She may also expect public assistance in the form of welfare. If you are thinking about this possibility, read Chapters 10 and 11. You are making plans for both your future and the future of your child.

Very often, there is an older sister who had a baby and they are both now living in the family. Chrissy tells us about the argument she had with her mother.

> *I have four sisters. I'm 15 and the youngest.*
> *Last year, Carrie, who was 16 years old, had a*
> *baby. So now I'm pregnant and I don't want an*
> *abortion. That's what my mom wants. She*
> *treats me differently from Carrie. She allowed*
> *her to have a baby, so why not me? It's no big*
> *deal. There's plenty of room. Mom is always*

complaining, "There's not enough food. We don't have enough money." Well, that's not true. We can get public assistance.

Chrissy is using her pregnancy as a bargaining point with her mother. She may win this argument, but what about the baby's future? At the moment, Chrissy is thinking more about herself and what she can gain by continuing the pregnancy, not about what she can give a growing, dependent child. Sometimes, a girl will want to have a baby as a means of *separating from her parents*; or as a way of withdrawing from the painful process of growing up. Others may see having a baby as an accomplishment, of making something of themselves.

At this point in a young woman's life, she may not see what the options are for her future or for her own personal development. However, if you think you are pregnant, or if you are in fact pregnant, you must be truthful with yourself. It is vital to you and your baby that you receive help and care immediately. Dealing with your pregnancy will be easier when you've come to understand what your goals are for your future and what your options are right now. You will have to act soon. An unexpected pregnancy will not just go away.

What You Can Do

The dilemma of being a pregnant teenager may seem overwhelming. Yet the problem of what to do can be broken down into small pieces. By looking at your situation one piece at a time, you can arrive at a way to find someone to confide in and someone to help you.

There are five basic steps involved in making a sound decision, whether that decision is big or small. The same steps apply to what to do about your own pregnancy.

1) Learn what your choices are.
2) Figure out the positive and negative aspects of each choice.

3) Choose one.
4) Act on your choice.
5) Accept both the positives and negatives of your choice in order to live comfortably with your decision.

When you are reading about other teenagers' experiences with abortion, adoption, and raising a baby, imagine yourself in their places. Try on the different roles, see which one fits you best.

Some young women have a strong sense about what they will do if they are pregnant and confident they can carry out their decision alone. Others are not as sure. But whether you want to continue your pregnancy or not, don't make a snap decision. Don't let the urgency of your feelings push you into making a decision you can't live with later.

Make a list in your mind of the good things associated with each choice. Then consider the difficulties with each choice. Sometimes it helps to actually write down your thoughts and feelings about the decision you want to make. Confused emotions become much clearer when you put them down on paper.

There are several vitally important people to consider when making your decision.

* YOU—what is the best choice for you?
* Your baby—how will your decision ultimately affect the child growing within you?
* The baby's father—what are his wishes? Are you well suited enough to try to raise the baby together? Is marriage a possibility?
* Your parents—how will your decision affect them?

No matter how old you are, you should consider all the options open to you and try to make your final decision only after realistically exploring all aspects of that decision.

In the days and weeks to come, you will learn many new facts concerning pregnancy, abortion, and childbirth. Hopefully, you will also come away from this experience with a greater understanding of yourself, your feelings, and your goals for the future.

This is a difficult time for you. It is difficult for every young woman who thinks she may be pregnant. Try to learn from the experiences and feelings of others. And remember, you are not alone.

TWO

GOING ALL THE WAY

My first time was wonderful. I was in love with the man and he was so gentle and loving with me. Afterwards, we fell asleep together and he held me all night long. I felt very special. Sex after that just kept getting better.—Rita, 18.

My boyfriend and I smoked a couples of "Js" and drank a lot of beer. That's when I'd let him do it. My head was never really there. I just couldn't face dealing with it.—Joyce, 15.

Sex is no big deal. It's all right, but if I had my choice, I wouldn't do it as often as my boyfriend wants me to. You know how it is, though, it's not cool to say no.—Sandra, 16.

"Everybody Is Doing It"

Being in love with someone and having the desire to be close with him; having strong sexual feelings and wanting to express them with another person; wanting to explore and learn what sex is all about; hoping to be liked and popular—these are some of the reasons a girl might want to go all the way with a boy.

Kissing, hugging, touching, necking, and petting feel good. Making love can be a beautiful experience. Almost everyone longs to share feelings of closeness and joy, and to receive total acceptance from another person.

Sex and love are wonderful when they go together. But sometimes young people, and even adults, have trouble combining them. Physical sex and emotional love get all mixed up.

Many teenagers do not want to have intercourse, they just need to be held. They like cuddling and having somebody care about them. They enjoy the feeling of romance. Sometimes they have sex hoping to find love.

Katie, 17, is not a typical example, but she does express the strong need that people have to give and receive love.

> *My father died when I was twelve and my mother died just as I turned 17. I was scared and lonely and needed love. I began dating a man I had known for about six years. I had always had a crush on him. After we had sex, I thought I had to love him, but I didn't. I know that now. I looked for love in the wrong places.*

Sometimes, a teenager has a boyfriend who is a few years older than she. He might have a job, or be in college. When you don't have very much money, having a boyfriend who buys you things or takes you to dinner or the movies can be exciting. The young man then becomes the provider of the material things a teenage girl likes to have. He might also give her social status. By dating him, she becomes more popular and more accepted. Having sexual intercourse with him is part of the "unspoken deal" in the relationship. It's an old saying—"A man expects to pay for the date, a woman is expected to pay with sex."

Very often, a girl will have sex to hold on to a boy. She is afraid that he will leave her if she doesn't go all the way with him.

> *My boyfriend really pressured me into doing it. I knew that he had been making it with his last girlfriend and now he expected me to do the same. He just about told me outright that if I didn't, he'd look for someone else who would. I wanted to keep him, so I did.—Wendy, 15.*

Sometimes, especially for girls just entering their teens, having intercourse is merely a continuation of childhood sex play. Many younger teenagers are simply enjoying the touching and exploring games they have had with the boys they grew up with.

For other people, sexual activity is expected to start early and is generally accepted by the community.

> *We all started having sex when we were about 13 or 14. Look, it was a small town in the middle of nowhere and we had nothing else to do. Saturday nights we'd get in a car, down some beer and screw. Half the girls in my graduating class were pregnant. But that's all we had to do. Drinking, driving, and doing it.*

Another major reason young people have intercourse is to establish their sexual identity. Sex is also a way to feel independent, to begin to separate psychologically from parents and become your own person. Having sex with someone is like taking a leaping jump into adulthood. Having sex for the first time is an important moment in a teenager's life, a crossing of the border between childhood and adulthood.

Ronnie, who is 16, expresses her feelings about having sex for the first time.

> *Finally I knew what all the adults were whispering about. I learned what the secret of sex was. Suddenly, I felt like I was their equal. I wasn't just a dumb kid anymore. I had joined the ranks of being a grown-up.*

Today, there is a tremendous amount of pressure on a teenage girl to have sex. It comes from the rapid hormonal changes of adolescence, from the emotional need to be loved and accepted, from boys and men who have their own pressures and needs, and from the media. Television, radio, advertisements, movies, magazines, and music bombard people with sexual information. They tell you how you should look, and how you should behave. The media implies that you should wear sexy clothes and be tantalizing.

Everything around you and inside you seems to be shouting, "Be sexual!" It affects you, your friends, and young people across the nation. Some studies show that up to half of America's teenagers have had sex between the ages of 13 and 19. The average age of the first sexual encounter for a girl is 16. And by the age of 18, two out of three girls have gone all the way with a boy. It seems that "everybody is doing it."

"What's So Great About Sex?"

Teenage girls have many reactions to having sex. Some young women find it pleasurable and an expression of affection, others think it's great fun and a release of sexual tension. Still others are uncomfortable having sex and don't like it very much. Some teenage girls have deep feelings for the boy and therefore feel comfortable being sexual with him. Others do it because it's what the boy wants.

Quite a few girls share the feelings Melanie, 19, has.

> *I was sexually active at 16, but I wasn't getting anything out of it. I was saying, "What's so great about sex? What's so wonderful about this? I'm not getting satisfied."*

Many young people feel that the actual experience of sexual intercourse is not all that fantastic.

> *After my first time, while we were driving home, I kept thinking, "Is that all there is?" My boyfriend said it was the greatest. I pretended that I thought it was, too, but inside I was wondering if I was the only person who didn't, you know, come during sex. I thought there was something wrong with me.—Barbara, 17.*

Not every teenage girl experiences an orgasm the first time she has sex. Many women report that they have trouble achieving an orgasm the first time with a new man. This is not unusual. Some girls have orgasms during their teens, others don't. All girls have the ability to have orgasms.

Sometimes, though, the first sexual experience with somebody causes too much tension and anxiety for a girl to have an orgasm. If she is worried about getting pregnant, that may also keep her from responding fully.

Frequently, the reason a girl does not have an orgasm is because her partner comes too quickly or does not know what pleases her sexually. Often, it just takes a while to get attuned to each other's bodies and desires, as well as becoming comfortable enough with each other to share feelings about what is pleasurable and what is not.

Another reason why young women don't enjoy going all the way is the guilt and shame they feel about being sexual.

> *I was going to be married in two months when I had sex for the first time with my husband-to-be. Afterwards, I felt smutty, you know, dirty. I felt like I had done something really wrong. Even though I was about to be married, I still felt that way. I couldn't help it.—Donna, 19.*

Having sex for the first time is a deep personal experience. It takes time to absorb what has happened and to sort out your feelings about it. For many girls and women, it may take weeks, months, or years to feel totally comfortable about being a sexual person. Accepting yourself as you are, including your sexuality, is part of growing up.

Understanding Boys

Trying to understand boys is another part of growing up. When it comes to sex, boys are obviously different from girls, at least anatomically. The reasons a boy might want to go all the way are often the same—he longs to be touched and loved and accepted just as a girl does.

Girls want to explore their own sexuality just as much as boys want to explore theirs. Having sex for a boy is part of the same process of achieving a sexual identity and of beginning to separate from his parents. Just as you want to establish your femininity, a boy wants to establish his masculinity.

But there are some differences and one of them is the way a boy reacts to the sexual pressures around him and the hormones that are surging within him.

The peer pressure to go all the way with a girl is very strong for a boy. If a boy doesn't, he might be accused of being a "sissy" or a "fag." A boy faces a lot of ribbing and ridicule by remaining a virgin.

Many boys brag about how far they've gone. Some make up stories about their sexual experience. For these teenagers, scoring with a girl is a way to achieve prestige and respect from their friends. To a great number of boys, having sex reassures them that they are not different from other boys.

Furthermore, boys are bombarded with sexual stimuli. Seductive television shows, sexy songs, girlie magazines—a boy can become aroused just thinking about girls. Then, being very close with a real girl, touching her, kissing her, petting with her, is often sexually overwhelming. It is all so new and exciting that he may have difficulty controlling his impulses and his body.

Many teenage boys are embarrassed when they get a hard-on at the wrong time or place. Sometimes a boy will feel like coming just by looking at pictures of nude girls, or by being near someone who excites him.

The hormones released into a boy's body during adolescence can have a powerful and unsettling effect. His desire to go all the way with a girl may be experienced as an urgent need to release sexual tension. Because his penis is an external organ, easily seen, touched, and stimulated, his sexual feelings are concentrated in this area. His body achieves sexual release through orgasm and ejaculation.

Sexual feelings are somewhat different for a girl. Though she has a special organ, the clitoris, where sexual sensations are concentrated, these feelings are also diffused throughout her entire body. It may take longer for her to be stimulated to the same level as her partner. This is achieved through being held and kissed, and through being stroked and touched on all parts of her body, including the clitoris, vulva, and vagina.

Understanding your own sexual feelings and how boys react to their sexual feelings can help you to cope with the possibility of going all the way.

The Lines Boys Use

Some young men are genuinely in love with a girl and want to express their caring and affection sexually. However, some teenage boys (and some adult men) will try to manipulate a girl in order to achieve sexual satisfaction.

Here are just some of the lines that a boy might use to persuade you to go to bed with him.

"If you really loved me, you'd do it."
"I need you. Let me do it just this one time."
"You can't get pregnant. I'm sure I'm sterile."
"You're such a baby. Why don't you grow up?"
"No girl has ever gotten me this excited before."
"If you get pregnant, I'll marry you."
"What if there was a nuclear war tomorrow? You'll have died without ever experiencing sex."
"I heard you were frigid."
"I'll leave you if you don't."
"Relax, I've never gotten anybody else pregnant."
"You know you want it just as much as I do."
"Nobody has to know about it. This is just between you and me.
"Sex will bring us closer together."
"If we don't, I'll have a permanent injury."

There must be thousands of variations on "the line." Beware and recognize a line when you hear it. Remember, *you* are the only one who should decide whether you want to have sex or not.

When Sex Can Be Hurtful

As we have seen, sex can bring pleasure and a wonderful feeling of closeness and belonging. But it can also bring on confusing feelings, hurt feelings, and even painful feelings—especially if you get pregnant.

If you are wrestling with the many growing up tasks of adolescence, such as achieving independence from your parents, establishing your own identity, and deciding on a career goal, you're probably asking yourself questions like, "Who am I?" "What do I want to be?" "How do I come across to boys?" "Will they like me?" You may feel that having a sexual relationship with a boy will help to answer some of these questions. Instead, you may find yourself feeling more lost and confused by a relationship you don't feel ready for. This could delay or even stop the process of finding yourself.

For some young women, penetration by a boy's penis is frightening. It's an invasion of their bodies. Nanci, 17, relates her first experience.

> *When my boyfriend pulled out his cock, I suddenly got scared. "No way are you putting that thing in me," I told him. Well, I didn't let him that night, but soon after I went all the way with him and it was awful. It hurt and I bled. I never wanted to see him again. We broke up after that.*

Sometimes a girl can get hurt because a boy she cares about is just using her for his own pleasure. If this happens to you, you may feel bad about yourself because you are being treated like an object. You may also feel angry because you do not experience the same pleasure that the boy does. Sex can then become a negative experience for you.

Using alcohol or drugs may result in someone being able to persuade you to do something you wouldn't do if you were straight.

I got drunk one night and lost my virginity. My boyfriend and me were drinking vodka straight out of the bottle at a party. I was so stoned, I couldn't see anymore. We were kissing and petting and you know . . . before I knew it, he had it in me.—Alicia, 15.

You can also hurt someone else by having sex. For example, pretending to love a boy when you don't, messing around with someone else's boyfriend or husband, lying about sex with somebody else, or using sex to get something from another person.

Being forced to have sex when you don't want to is a very painful experience. Judy, 16, tells what happened to her.

I had been dating my boyfriend for a while and we had been getting pretty close to going all the way. Then one night while we were parking, and we were in the back seat of his car, he decided he wanted to do it. I was screaming at the top of my lungs that I didn't want to, but he forced me. I was crying so hard and I felt so ashamed. But I thought I really liked him, so we did it again next time. I probably did it about eight times with him, then he dropped me. I wasn't cool about sex, he said, and he had other girlfriends.

It is possible that a man will not understand, or will choose not to understand, a woman's protests. Because she may have been involved with him, gradually going from kissing to necking to heavy petting, he may believe that full sexual intercourse is the next step and may in fact demand it. Some men can become quite manipulative and even threatening in order to get what they want.

No act of lovemaking should involve physical force. But, unfortunately, this is sometimes the case. Rape is a crime that involves forcible sexual intercourse against a woman's will. If a man hits a woman, overpowers her, uses, or threatens to use a weapon, such as a knife or a gun, she may have no choice but to do what the rapist wants in order to stay unhurt and alive. In this case, rape is not a sexual act but an act of violence. It can be done by a stranger, a relative, an acquaintance, or a boyfriend. In any case, it can be a shattering experience and should be reported to the police as soon as possible. Many police stations have policewomen who handle rape cases.

A rape victim will also be treated by a doctor, who can provide treatment for venereal disease. In addition, he or she may discuss the possibility of taking a "morning after pill," which is a very strong hormone, to prevent a pregnancy from occurring. Becoming pregnant as a result of rape can be particularly devastating. Some people, who are otherwise opposed to abortion, feel that it is justified in the case of rape.

Rape leaves a woman feeling hurt both physically and emotionally. She may feel violated and powerless. Her sense of personal security and safety have been shattered. Afterward, a rape victim can feel she has lost control of her life and her body: that the boundaries of her very being have been broken and destroyed. Many victims replay the event in their memories, trying to regain control of the situation, even to the point of blaming themselves. As a result, women who have been raped live with feelings of fear, anxiety, humiliation, guilt, and rage. Speaking with someone who counsels rape victims can help them overcome these painful feelings and gain some understanding of what has happened. There are counseling groups for rape victims in most cities and communities. The police should be able to put you in touch with one.

What About Birth Control?

Caring for and respecting the other person are important elements in a healthy sexual relationship. Planning for sex by using birth control is also important.

You probably know something already about birth control. Perhaps you've had a class in school that taught you about the various ways of preventing pregnancy. Many teenagers say that they know all about birth control.

Yet, most teenagers who have sex do not use any reliable form of birth control. Why?

There are several reasons. The need for privacy is one. Sex is very personal. It's not the kind of subject you can discuss with just anybody. Even though birth control is available to teenagers, many hesitate to get it because they are embarrassed to go to a clinic or a doctor.

> *I had been going all the way with my boyfriend for several months. I knew I should be on the Pill, but I was too ashamed to go to a doctor. I didn't want him to think I was a whore.—Bette, 15.*

If you are having sex or are thinking about it, and are not yet ready for parenthood, getting birth control and using it properly is vital. Most health clinics will help you choose a method that works best for you and will support you in your decision to have responsible sex. There are numerous agencies that can help you. You will find a list with phone numbers at the back of this book. If you are thinking about having sex for the first time, or if you are already going all the way with a boy, make that phone call soon.

If you think you are pregnant, consult the back of this book as well. Telephone a health clinic or a doctor as soon as possible. You will need to speak with someone about how to get a pregnancy test.

Sometimes, a teenager's mother realizes her daughter is sexually active. If this is the case with you, your mother may want to talk to you about it, or go with you to a clinic. Sexual feelings may be hard enough to share with a girlfriend, let alone a parent. You may feel the need to keep this part of your life private. Your sexuality is *yours,* not your mother's.

The feelings of the following two girls are typical. Perhaps you've felt the same way.

> *You know, I can talk to my mother about every- thing, but this is between Glenn and me. This I just can't talk to her about. We can talk about*

sex and birth control in theory. But what I do sexually is something else. I don't want her to know everything about my private life.— Yvonne, 16.

My mother said to me, "If you're having sex, tell me and we'll go to my gynecologist and get you birth control pills." I told her to get out of my life. "Bug off, Mom," I said, "you don't have control over this part of me. I am an individual and this is my body. You can't treat me like a child anymore. You have to deal with me as an adult."—Julia, 18.

Your mother might be baffled and hurt by feelings like these. Yet as difficult as this is for your mother to understand, reactions such as Yvonne's and Julia's are normal. They are part of the process of separating from parents during the adolescent years.

Since sex and birth control are usually kept private by a young person, you might not get the contraceptives you need because you don't know *where* to go, how to get there, or whether a clinic will help someone your age. The clinics listed in the back of this book can answer these and other questions you might have.

There are many reasons why young people fail to use reliable birth control. There has been much negative publicity concerning possible health risks of the Pill. Young women fear cancer, strokes, and heart attacks, even though the risk is extremely small for healthy young women. The possible side effects associated with taking birth control pills, such as weight gain, headaches, nausea, vaginal infections, or depression, will also keep many young people from trying, or staying with, this method. In fact, most doctors feel that the Pill is one of the safest, simplest, and most effective birth control methods available for teenagers.

The I.U.D. also requires a visit to a doctor. The idea of inserting anything up inside your body may be frightening. The side effects associated with this method—cramps and heavy bleeding—may make the I.U.D. an unpopular choice for birth control among teenagers. Many physicians are hesitant to prescribe an I.U.D. for a young woman who has not had children because of possible infection, embedding, perforation, or build up of scar tissue.

Using a diaphragm or spermicidal foam is often rejected by girls who are uncomfortable about touching their own bodies. Most girls have never looked at their sexual organs and many have been taught that it's shameful and dirty "down there." It takes knowledge of your own body and some practice to properly use these methods. Most teenagers have neither.

The rhythm method works best when your period is regular and you have a very good understanding about how the menstrual cycle works. This method involves careful planning and abstinence (no sexual intercourse) for a considerable amount of time each month.

Relying on your boyfriend to withdraw is also risky even though this is a popular method with teenagers. Very often a boy will come too fast and won't be able to pull out in time. He may also be so sexually excited that he may forget to withdraw. Furthermore, there is a clear fluid that can come out of the penis before ejaculation which contains sperm. Unhappily, this can result in an unwanted pregnancy for you.

Condoms, or rubbers, are an excellent birth control method that has fallen out of favor, especially with boys. They assume that it's the girl's responsibility to prevent pregnancy. Also, a boy may be embarrassed to ask for or buy condoms in a drug store. He may not realize that it can be just as embarrassing for a girl to obtain birth control and it's often more difficult for her. Yet the condom, especially if used in conjunction with a spermicidal foam inserted in the vagina, is almost as effective as the Pill in preventing pregnancies. Furthermore, the condom is the only birth control method that can also prevent venereal disease.

A great number of young people don't protect themselves because they don't make the connection that what they do today will affect them tomorrow. Most girls who become pregnant say, "I didn't think anything would happen." or "I didn't think this would happen to *me*."

Deep inside, many teenagers believe that having sex is wrong. If you don't plan for it by arranging for birth control ahead of time, then you can say to yourself, "It wasn't my fault. It just happened." or "I was carried away. I never meant to go that far." You didn't *plan* to be "bad," therefore you are still good.

Still other young women think that sex should be romantic and spontaneous. Planning for it in advance would seem cold and calculating.

There is nothing romantic about finding yourself pregnant when you don't want to be. Having sex opens up the possibility of getting pregnant. It happens to four out of five girls who have unprotected sex, and it can happen to girls who use birth control only once in a while. Most teenagers become pregnant within six months of their first sexual encounter.

In conclusion, having sexual feelings is part of the human experience. It is normal and natural. But having a sexual relationship carries responsibilities. You can hurt people with sex, and you can be hurt by sex. Because of this, many teenagers postpone going all the way until they are older and better equipped to handle the emotional and realistic aspects of sex. For both men and women, a responsible sexual relationship means caring—caring for your partner and caring for yourself enough to use birth control to prevent an unplanned pregnancy.

THREE

IF YOU THINK YOU'RE PREGNANT

I became more and more scared as the weeks passed by and my period didn't come. Thinking about being pregnant was all I was doing. I couldn't concentrate on school or anything. I can't believe that my parents didn't know.—Debbie, 16.

At first I was worried when my period didn't come. Then I just started feeling happier and happier. I can't wait to have my baby and have someone to love me.—Freida, 15.

My period was 28 days late, but I'm always irregular. Then I felt nauseous and I had these cramps, so I thought my period was going to start any day. I didn't know that this is one of the signs of pregnancy.—Karen, 18.

How You Get Pregnant

It can happen to anyone, including you. Let's take a look at how the body works to understand how you can get pregnant and why it can so easily happen to you.

Between the ages of 9 and 18, a woman begins to menstruate. This is a normal part of growing up. In girls, the first period, called the menarche, signals the beginning of adolescence. A menstrual period will occur every 21 to 40 days. The average woman has a period every 28 days, but it's perfectly normal to have a period every 24 days, every 36 days, or to be irregular. Each period lasts about 3 to 7 days. Most women continue to have periods until they are between the ages of 45 and 55, which is when menopause begins.

The female body has two ovaries that produce eggs (ova). Once during each menstrual cycle, at the time approximately half way between your periods, one ovary will release one egg. It travels down through the fallopian tube where it can be fertilized by a male's sperm. Meanwhile, your uterus has been building up a lining to nourish the fertilized egg. If the egg is not fertilized, it simply dissolves and passes out of your body through the "os," the small opening of the cervix. About two weeks later, you will have a menstrual period, which is the shedding of the lining, since it is not needed that month. The whole process then repeats itself.

If an egg is fertilized by a male's sperm, conception (pregnancy) has occurred. Sperm enters a woman's body when a man ejaculates into or near her vagina. Semen, which contains millions of sperm, is the milky fluid that comes out of the man's penis when he has an orgasm. Within seconds, the sperm swim up into the uterus and into the fallopian tubes that connect the uterus to the ovaries. If an egg is present, one sperm will join with it and fertilize it.

After fertilization, the egg divides into two cells, then four cells, then eight cells, and so on, until it has formed a tiny ball. It continues to divide and grow as it travels down to the uterus where it implants itself into the lining the uterus has prepared. Since the lining is now needed to support and feed the embryo, there will no longer be a normal period for the duration of your pregnancy.

You can become pregnant if:

- You have had sexual intercourse with a man and were not using birth control.

- You have had sexual intercourse with a man and did not use birth control properly or the birth control method failed.

- The man ejaculated near the lips of your vagina and some sperm swam up to the Fallopian tubes.

Using birth control *consistently and correctly* will prevent conception with various high degrees of effectiveness.

Method	Effectiveness if used perfectly all the time	Effectiveness as used by actual couples
Pill	99+%	90-96%
I.U.D.	97-99%	95%
Diaphragm	97%	83%
Foam	97%	78%
Condom	97%	90%
Condom & Foam	99+%	95%
Rhythm	87%	79%
Withdrawal	91%	75-80%

As you can see, no birth control method can give you 100 percent protection all the time. By using birth control, though, you have a much better chance of avoiding an unexpected pregnancy. Most certainly, if you are a healthy young woman and you have had sexual intercourse, you can become pregnant if you used no birth control method at all.

"You Can't Get Pregnant If . . ."

There are many myths and misunderstandings concerning pregnancy. Let's get to the truth of some of them.

- You have to have your period for a few years before you can get pregnant.

FALSE. A girl can get pregnant right after her very first period.

Most often, a girl cannot become pregnant until she has had several periods, but not always. Each young woman is different. Some can get pregnant right after menarche, some not. There is no way *you* can tell for sure.

- You can't get pregnant during your period.

FALSE. You can get pregnant during your period. Your chances of getting pregnant are reduced during your period since most of the time, your ovaries will produce an egg only once during the middle of your cycle. Sometimes, however, your body may produce an additional egg during your period. There is no one time during the month that you are 100 percent safe.

- You can't get pregnant the first time.

FALSE. You can get pregnant the first time and many girls do. Your ovaries and the egg that is released don't know that this is your first time. If a sperm meets with an egg, it will be fertilized no matter how many times you've had sex.

- If he pulls out in time, you won't get pregnant.

FALSE. You can get pregnant even if your boyfriend pulls out in time. There are two reasons for this. Number one: A small drop of clear fluid, which can contain sperm, may escape from a man's penis while he is inside of you. He cannot tell that this has happened and neither can you. Number two: If a man comes, or ejaculates, anywhere near the vagina, some of his sperm may have already traveled up past your cervix and into your uterus.

- If you have an orgasm, you won't get pregnant.
- If you *don't* have an orgasm, you won't get pregnant.

FALSE. A woman's orgasm has no effect on her ability to get pregnant. A man must have an orgasm in order to release his sperm. But a woman's ovaries will produce an egg every month whether she has orgasms or not.

- You can only get pregnant in the missionary position. (That is, with the man on top.)

FALSE. You can get pregnant in *any* position. Some positions allow the man to ejaculate his semen deeper into the vagina, but usually this doesn't matter since sperm can travel to your fallopian tubes within seconds, no matter what position your body is in.

- If you douche after having sex, you can't get pregnant.

FALSE. Douching will not prevent conception. When a man has ejaculated in or near your vagina, his sperm swim extremely fast up into your body. As we already pointed out, in only a few seconds, some of his sperm have already passed through the opening in your cervix and are in your fallopian tubes. It doesn't matter what you douche with or when. Douching is *not* a form of birth control.

- I'm too young to get pregnant.

FALSE. If you have had one menstrual period, there is a chance you can get pregnant if you have intercourse with a man. Cases have been recorded of girls who became pregnant when they were only nine years old.

As you see, your chances of getting pregnant are high. There is great pressure on you to have sexual intercourse—from your friends, your boyfriend, your own feelings and needs. Getting birth control can seem embarrassing and using it may be difficult. Very often it just seems easier not to think about the future.

> *I figured if I didn't think about it, it wouldn't happen to me. But it did.—Elena, 17.*

If you have gone all the way with a boy, prepare yourself for the possibility of pregnancy. It happens to over a million girls each year. It can happen to you.

The Signs of Pregnancy

There are many signs of pregnancy. Sometimes they can be felt as early as a few days after conception. Most of the time, though, women begin to experience the symptoms of pregnancy several weeks later.

A missed period is usually the first sign and is often accompanied by other changes in your body. Let's take a look at what they are.

- *You have missed your period.* This is usually the earliest and most common indication of pregnancy. Sometimes, you may miss a period because of illness, malnutrition, stress, excessive dieting, or emotional trauma. Most often though, if you have had sexual intercourse with a boy, a missed period means that you are pregnant.

- *Your last period was not normal.* Sometimes a woman may be pregnant even though she still has what appears to be a menstrual period. These periods, though, are scantier and last fewer days or last only a few hours. The color of your period may seem different. In any case, if your last period did not seem normal, you may be pregnant.

- *You have cramps or abdominal pain.* Very often a pregnant woman will have cramps that feel as if her period is about to start. The cramps or pain will last for several days and then stop. If a normal period has not started, you may be pregnant.

- *Your breasts feel tender and they seem larger.* Your breasts begin to feel tender or even painful to touch. You might notice a tingling sensation. Your nipples might seem very sensitive and easily irritated. Furthermore, your breasts may seem fuller and enlarged.

- *You feel nauseous and/or are throwing up.* Nausea and vomiting during pregnancy are usually called "morning sickness," although they can occur at any time of the day or can last all day long.

- *Your eating habits change.* Some women lose their appetites when they become pregnant. The sight or smell of food or of certain foods make them feel ill. Other women feel like eating all the time or get cravings for a particular type of food.
- *You feel very tired.* Many women who are pregnant feel lethargic, as if they just have no energy. Sometimes, the need to sleep is powerful. You may have trouble getting up in the morning or you may feel like falling asleep during the day or early in the evening.
- *You seem to be gaining weight.* Another symptom of pregnancy is weight gain and thickening of the waist. Clothes may seem tighter. Your jeans may not zip up anymore. Some women experience a rather sudden "blowing-up" of the stomach. Your abdomen may feel rounder and fuller.
- *Some other symptoms.* Some of the other signs of pregnancy include the need to urinate more often, losing weight, backaches, pain in the legs, headaches, and dizziness.

These are all symptoms of pregnancy. You might experience many of these or just one or two of them. If you have gone all the way with a boy, whether or not you were using birth control, and you are experiencing any of the above symptoms, you may be pregnant.

"How Can I Get a Pregnancy Test?"

If you are experiencing the signs of pregnancy, it is important to have a pregnancy test done as soon as possible.

Perhaps you know of a neighborhood clinic or of a nearby hospital. If you have told someone about your suspected pregnancy, he or she might be able to suggest a place where you can get a pregnancy test.

If you don't know where to go, refer to the Yellow Pages in your phone book under "Birth Control Information Centers," "Clinics," and "Hospitals." You can get a pregnancy test at any gynecological clinic and at any hospital. Parental consent is not needed.

It is possible that there is no clinic or hospital nearby, or that your town does not have information or services for a teenager. You should then find a clinic in another town or city. Some girls prefer to go to another town because they would be embarrassed if they met anyone they knew while getting a pregnancy test.

If there is public transportation in your community, perhaps a bus or a train can take you to a clinic. If not, you will then need to turn to somebody you know who can provide you with transportation to a pregnancy testing center. You might be able to tell an older brother or sister, a friend with a car, a teacher or a school counselor, or any adult who can help. This might be the time to tell your mother or father.

If you don't want your parents to know just yet, wait until you are alone in the house to call the clinic or place the call at a local pay phone. Take several dimes with you and a pen and paper to write down the information you are given.

When you make your phone call, tell the person who answers about your situation. You might want to say something like, "Hello. I'm ____ years old and I think I might be pregnant. I'd like to make an appointment for a pregnancy test."

You will be given an appointment or be transferred to someone in the adolescent department of the hospital or clinic. You might also be referred to another clinic or hospital that can provide better services for you.

Be prepared to answer any questions that the receptionist asks you such as, "When was your last normal period?" or "Are you experiencing any other symptoms?"

You might have some questions you want to ask. Feel free to inquire about anything you don't know or don't understand. Be sure to ask about costs. Some clinics and hospitals offer free pregnancy testing. Others might charge five or ten dollars.

Most clinics, hospitals and private doctors will want to be paid in cash, or with a money order or a traveler's check. (Some clinics will take major credit cards.) Try to find a clinic or a hospital which provides free pregnancy testing. If you have no money, explain this to the receptionist. Most clinics and some hospitals will make an exception in the case of a teenager. If the clinic or hospital insists on being paid, however, and you can't find a free clinic in your area, you will have to find a way to come up with the money. Perhaps a friend or a relative can loan you the money. Is there someone at school you can confide in about this? If you still can't find a way to pay for the pregnancy test, have the hospital or clinic refer you to a social worker. He or she should be able to help you arrange for a pregnancy test and any follow-up care you may need.

If the response you get at the first clinic or hospital you call seems cold to you or not just right, thank the person to whom you are talking, hang up, and try the next one on your list. Most organizations want to be helpful to you, but you must decide which one you feel most comfortable with.

Pregnancy testing is often done only during certain hours. Try to make the appointment for the day and the time that is most convenient for you. Write down the exact time, date, and place for your appointment. Most clinics and hospitals have very busy schedules, so do your best to be on time for your appointment.

The Pregnancy Test

A pregnancy test determines whether or not a pregnancy hormone is present in your body. The hormone, which is produced during pregnancy, is called human chorionic gonadotropin, or HCG. It can be found in your blood and in your urine if you are pregnant.

Usually, the simple urine test is used to detect HCG if your period is more than two weeks late.

On the day of your appointment with a doctor or a clinic, you will be asked to bring in a first morning urine specimen. The hormone is most concentrated after a night's sleep and therefore can be more accurately detected.

When you wake up that morning, take a clean jar into the bathroom with you. Urinate directly into the jar and then close the lid securely on the jar. Take this jar with you to the clinic or hospital. If it is difficult for you to accomplish this in your home, a urine sample can be taken at the clinic.

The urine test is about 98 percent accurate, and you usually can learn the results the same day.

If your period is less than two weeks late or not yet late, and you are experiencing some of the other signs of pregnancy, a blood test can be taken. A blood test determines the presence of HCG ten days after conception. A blood test might also be taken if your periods are irregular or if the urine test result was negative but you are still experiencing other symptoms of pregnancy. This type of test usually costs between $10 and $25.

The blood test is 99 percent accurate and can be done in a clinic or doctor's office. A small sample of blood is taken from your arm and the blood must then be analyzed in a laboratory. Results usually can be obtained within 24 to 48 hours.

Home pregnancy tests are now available. They can be purchased in most drug stores for about $10. The results can be learned in about twenty minutes in the privacy of your own home. The test is basically the same urine test that is used by doctors and clinics; however, there is a greater chance of inaccuracy. You might get a false reading. If you think you are pregnant, whether you actually are nor not, it's a good idea to make an appointment with a counselor or a physician to talk either about birth control or about your pregnancy.

The Pregnancy Test Is *Negative*

If the test is *negative,* you are probably *not pregnant.* We say probably because sometimes it is possible to have a "false negative" reading. This is especially true of the urine test. A "false negative" can happen if your period is less than two weeks late. Even a day too early can make a difference. This can also happen if your urine sample was taken later in the day. The pregnancy hormone may not have been concentrated enough. A blood test may show a "false negative" if you are less than ten days pregnant.

Should you receive a negative result and your period has still not started after one week, go back to the clinic or hospital for a second test. If that test is again negative, you should see a physician for an internal pelvic examination to determine if you are pregnant.

The Pregnancy Test Is *Positive*

If the pregnancy test is *positive,* it means that you are *most likely pregnant.* Though it is extremely rare, a "false positive" can occur because of certain drugs or medications you are taking, or because of certain tumors on the ovaries.

Should your pregnancy test be positive, it is recommended that you have a pelvic examination. A pelvic exam can confirm your pregnancy and can indicate how many weeks pregnant you are. This information is vital to you whether you decide to have an abortion or whether you want to continue your pregnancy.

The Pelvic Exam

Many teenagers have their first pelvic examination when they become pregnant. The thought of having a pelvic exam makes many people feel nervous and uneasy. It takes some time to become comfortable with the idea of a doctor or a clinician touching and examining you in a place that is so private.

> *I was more scared of the pelvic exam than I was of finding out I was pregnant. I must have been shaking from head to toe when I went into the examining room.—Pam, 15.*

These nervous and scared feelings are natural. The pelvic exam can be especially frightening if you don't know what's going to happen. Finding out what will be done during a pelvic exam, and why it needs to be done, will help you to feel more relaxed and at ease during the examination. You might even be able to use this experience to learn more about your own body and about yourself.

I was nervous before the pelvic exam, but afterwards, it felt really good to know that I was normal and that all my parts were healthy and working. This was the first time I had ever been to a doctor by myself and when I think about that and the fact that I got through the pelvic exam . . . well, I felt like I had really accomplished something.—Rena, 17.

A pelvic exam is done in order to:

1) make sure your sexual and reproductive organs are in good physical condition.
2) check for any infections that might occur inside your vagina, uterus, or ovaries.
3) take a Pap smear which is a routine check for abnormal cells on your cervix.
4) confirm a pregnancy.
5) find out how many weeks pregnant you are.

A pelvic exam can cost between $25 and $75. The charge for a Pap smear or a test for V.D. is about $5 to $15. Treatment for an infection or venereal disease costs about $5 up to $20. If you think you may have trouble paying this amount, you might be able to get help from a friend or an adult, or you can try to find a clinic that either makes a fee arrangement or charges no fee for teenagers. Again, a social worker might be able to assist you.

This is a very important health examination. Don't let your nervousness or worries about money keep you from getting one. In fact, a sexually active woman should have a pelvic exam once a year whether or not she is pregnant. Millions of women have them every year. It is a simple and easy procedure which doesn't hurt.

Inside the Examination Room

The pelvic examination can be performed by a physician, by a trained physician's assistant, or by a nurse practitioner. These professionals might also be called "clinicians" or "practitioners" to simplify explanations.

Before you see the clinician, you will be taken to the examining room. There you will be asked to change into a cloth or paper cover-up "gown," which is provided for you to wear during the examination. Most examining rooms have a sectioned-off area where you can undress in privacy, or you will be left alone in the room until you are changed. After your cover-up gown is on, you may sit in a chair or on the examining table and wait for the clinician to enter.

Once the clinician has entered, he or she may ask you about your medical history—when you were born, what diseases or allergies you have had, any medications you might now be taking, and when you had your last normal menstrual period.

You will then be asked to lie down on the table so that your breasts can be examined. The practitioner may show you how to examine your own breasts—you should check them once a month. If you have any questions about your breasts, be sure to ask. And if you have noticed any thickening, soreness, or lumps in your breasts, let the practitioner know.

Now, on to the actual pelvic examination. You will be asked to put your feet in two holders, called stirrups, that are at the end of the table. You might also be asked to slide yourself down the table a little so that you are in a better position to be examined. Let your knees fall apart as naturally as possible. You might feel awkward in this position—most women do—but, so far, it's the only way that a clinician can check the reproductive parts of your body.

Many young women worry about pain once the pelvic exam begins. The pelvic exam usually causes a feeling of pressure, but it should not hurt. If you do feel a distinct soreness or pain, tell your doctor right away. The pelvic exam itself should cause no pain.

It can be difficult to relax, especially if this is your first pelvic exam. It will help to place your hands comfortably on your chest and to breath deeply. Take a deep breath in with your nose, hold it a second, and then slowly breathe out with your mouth. Repeat this rhythmically until the examination is completed. It may also help to realize that the pelvic exam is a routine physical examination that the clinician does many times each day.

First, the practitioner will check the outside parts for any signs of swelling, irritation, or discharge. He or she might touch your thigh to let you get used to the feel of his or her hands touching you.

Then the clinician will put one or possibly two gloved fingers inside your vagina. With the other hand, the clinician will gently press down on your abdomen. In this way, your uterus and ovaries can be felt for size, shape, swelling, or tenderness. From the size of the uterus, a clinician can give a good estimate of how many weeks pregnant you are.

Usually, a practitioner will also place an instrument called a speculum into your vagina. The speculum holds the walls of the vagina apart, so that the practitioner can see the inside of your vagina and your cervix. Your cervix is usually pink or red in color; however, when you are pregnant, it becomes bluish in color because of the increase of blood supply to that region.

The clinician may then perform a Pap smear. To do this, he or she inserts a long cotton swab and gently dabs your cervix to collect the cells needed for the test, which is done in a laboratory.

If you suspect you might have a venereal disease ask the practitioner to do a V.D. test. Don't be embarrassed to ask. It's for your protection and health.

Remember, throughout this examination, you are allowed to ask questions. In fact, you should ask questions. Doctors and nurses need to work *with* you to give you the best medical care possible.

If You *Are* Pregnant

Following the pregnancy test and the pelvic exam, you will know for sure whether or not you are pregnant.

Learning that you are in fact pregnant can be a very important moment in your life. Some teenagers feel happy and relieved at the news.

> *I was so excited to find out that I was going to have a baby! My boyfriend said I could move in with him if I was pregnant and now we can start planning for our baby together.—Ami, 15.*

Many girls, though, feel numb and in shock.

> *When I telephoned the clinic and the nurse said "the test is positive," my mind went blank. I said something dumb like, "Does that mean I'm pregnant?" Then I just began to walk. I walked for a long time, not thinking clearly at all. It was as if my brain had just stopped.— Jessica, 18.*

To others, a positive pregnancy test just doesn't seem real.

> *How can this be? I don't feel any different. And now they're telling me I'm pregnant. I just can't believe it.—Jenny, 16.*

Many young women feel panicky and begin to cry. Some teenagers believe that getting pregnant is a punishment for having sex, while others are stunned. Many girls have said, "Why me? Everybody's doing it. How come I got caught?" Other reactions include depression, fear, and/or anger. You might be angry at your boyfriend or at yourself.

The important thing now is to try to sort out your feelings and to figure out what you want to do now that you are pregnant.

You may feel confused or overwhelmed by the news of your pregnancy. Yet you must now make a decision about how to proceed with your life.

You may already have a strong sense of what you will do. Margie, 17, feels confident that abortion is the right choice for her.

I'm not going to have a baby. I don't want a baby. I'm too young. I want to finish school. I have plans for a career. My boyfriend wants me to keep the baby, but tough on him. He caused this whole thing anyway.

Anita, 15, is going to keep her baby and try to raise it herself.

I want this baby more than anything. I think I will be a good mother. I know that I can give my baby plenty of love.

Camella, 19, is planning to marry her boyfriend.

My religion tells me abortion is wrong. I guess my boyfriend and I are both old-fashioned. He felt that he should marry me when I got pregnant. And I'm glad about that. I think our baby will grow up in a good, stable household.

Whether you know what you will do or still feel confused and undecided, learn as much as you can about the choices available to you before making your decision. It may be the most important decision of your life.

FOUR

TELLING THE IMPORTANT PEOPLE IN YOUR LIFE

When I first thought I might be pregnant, what I wanted to do most was tell my mom. I knew she would have some answers and be able to help me. But I didn't know how to say the words and I didn't know how she would react. I was scared she might get real angry at me. I needed her more than ever, but I was afraid to tell her.—Melissa, 14.

I didn't tell anybody until I got a pregnancy test and it was positive. Then I told my boyfriend. Let me tell you, that was not easy. He didn't want to hear about it. He said he didn't care what I did. Later, I told him I had an abortion. And he broke down and began to cry. I guess it affected him a lot more than he wanted to admit.—Nicole, 16.

The thought of being pregnant terrified me. I just couldn't tell my parents and I broke up with my boyfriend weeks ago. So I decided to tell my English teacher, who is a very nice, understanding person. She offered to take me to get a pregnancy test and then went with me to tell my parents. Being able to talk with them helped me make up my mind about what to do.—Michelle, 17.

Talking To Someone You Trust

An unexpected pregnancy is a difficult situation to handle all by yourself. At some point, you will probably want to talk to somebody in order to share your feelings and to get help in carrying out your decision about your pregnancy.

Most girls ultimately tell their boyfriends and their parents, but many talk to a girlfriend, a sister, a cousin, or someone at school first. It is natural to want to share your thoughts and feelings with someone close to your own age. Sometimes a friend can lead you to a clinic or someone else who can help you. Other times, though, a friend may give you wrong information. She might also accidently tell other people.

If you are confused about where to go for help, start with your school guidance counselor. You might also wish to talk to a school nurse, a health education teacher, or a gym coach. Try to talk to somebody with whom you can feel comfortable. What is important is to find an adult you feel you can trust and with whom you can share a confidence.

Should you want to talk to someone at your school, but are worried they will notify your parents, ask beforehand if he or she will keep your conversation private. You might say, "I'd like to talk to you about something serious, but I don't want my parents to know just yet. Can I talk to you confidentially?"

A counselor, nurse, or teacher might be able to help you find a family planning clinic or a hospital, and may be able to help you tell your parents, should you decide to do so.

If you have strong religious feelings, you may need to talk to your minister, priest, or rabbi. He or she can help you understand your feelings within the teachings of your particular religious belief. The support of your church or synagogue may be important to you in accepting and adjusting to your ultimate decision. Most religious organizations can refer you to social agencies, clinics, and other organizations that can assist a pregnant teenager.

Many young women report temporary feelings of loneliness, confusion, guilt, fear, or sadness. Sharing the news of your pregnancy can help to overcome these feelings and, at the same time, focus your thoughts on making a decision about the outcome of your pregnancy.   .

Yet feelings can be overwhelming, especially when you think you are all alone and have no one to talk to. When a young woman feels deeply troubled about other aspects of her life, pregnancy can make the problems seem worse. For a few teenagers, being pregnant brings on feelings of despair and, sometimes, thoughts of suicide.

If you feel hopeless, alone, and unable to cope with an unexpected pregnancy, call a teen hot line. The phone numbers of many hot lines are listed in the back of this book. If there is no hot line in your area, and you are feeling suicidal, tell a responsible adult, even if it is someone you don't know well, such as your employer, your school principal, a clergyperson, or even a friend's parent. If there is no one to turn to, go to the emergency room of the nearest hospital and simply say to the receptionist, "I am thinking about suicide. Please help me." You will receive immediate aid.

In general, if you need help with an unplanned pregnancy, check the back of this book for listings in your state. You might also want to look at the Yellow Pages in your telephone book. You'll find help under the headings of "Social Service Organizations," "Clinics," "Religious Organizations," "Clergy," and "Churches." In the White Pages, look for such well-known national organizations as Family Information Service, Planned Parenthood, Florence Crittenton, Jewish Welfare Federation, Lutheran Family and Children Services, American Red Cross, The Salvation Army, and YWCA.

Telling Your Boyfriend

How you feel about your boyfriend and how he feels about you and your pregnancy will undoubtedly influence the decision you make about the outcome of your pregnancy.

Most girls do tell their boyfriends, but some do not, for various reasons.

I didn't tell my boyfriend because I know he'd want me to have the baby. He'd get all worked up about his manhood and his "right" to the baby. I just want an abortion.—Rachel, 17.

My boyfriend? I hardly even knew the guy who got me pregnant. I don't know why I'd want to get him involved with this. It's my body and my decision.—Susan, 16.

However, if you and your boyfriend have an ongoing relationship, you will probably want him to share the decision making process. The best thing you can do is to be honest with him. Share your thoughts and feelings about your pregnancy—both positive and negative.

Many couples decide that abortion is right for them. Other young people decide to have the baby and raise it together while each remains living in their parents' home. Some try living together. Others choose to get married.

Sometimes, the crisis of an unexpected pregnancy will bring a couple closer together. The nature of the crisis provides an opportunity to share their deepest feelings about themselves and each other. Sharing a difficult experience tests the strength of the relationship. If feelings between you and your boyfriend are deep and meaningful, your relationship may grow stronger.

Expect your boyfriend to have feelings of his own. Often a boy has trouble expressing his true feelings openly. He may feel left out or believe that his feelings don't count or that he must be the strong one because *you* are the one who is pregnant. He may feel guilty because he "got you pregnant" and it's you who must go through either childbirth or abortion, while he bears no physical consequence for the pleasure of intercourse. He might feel obligated to see you through this experience. He might also be frightened because he has to face up to the possibility of contributing to the support of a baby until the child reaches maturity. Fatherhood can be very scary to someone who is not prepared for it.

Because a boy's participation in conceiving a baby begins and ends with intercourse, when his girlfriend becomes pregnant, he is likely to feel excluded, no matter what she decides.

The fact that you can decide to give birth or have an abortion without his agreement, leaves him feeling that he has no control over a situation that could affect the rest of his life. He may get angry if he is unable to influence your decision. Sometimes a boyfriend will try to "bully" his girlfriend into doing what he wants her to do. On the other hand, a boy might be so panicked by how his girlfriend's pregnancy could affect his life, that he runs away from the situation. He might stop calling or might even disappear from town.

The stress of an unwanted pregnancy can break a couple apart. It's a painful thing to have happen, especially at a time when you need emotional support. If this does happen to you, it helps to let yourself express whatever sad or angry feelings you have inside. Try to get the emotional support you need from a parent, a girlfriend, or anyone who will listen sympathetically.

Whether you and your boyfriend stay together or not, it's important to keep focused on your pregnancy and what you plan to do about it. You have to make a very serious decision about your pregnancy as well as carry it out.

The bottom line is that you should not do anything—have a baby, get an abortion, put your child up for adoption—to please a man or a boy. *You* must live with the consequence of your decision, so it's important to decide what's right for you and follow through with that. It's your life, your body, and your future.

"How Can I Tell My Parents?"

Some girls can talk to their parents about their personal problems. Experience has taught these teenagers that no matter how bad the news they bring, they can depend upon their parents to help them find a solution.

For others, talking with parents about personal things is extremely difficult. Telling them about a pregnancy might seem impossible.

*I can't tell my mom I'm pregnant. I can't even
talk to her about sex. She's going to be awfully
angry. I know she'll cry . . . then she'll force me
to stop seeing my boyfriend.—Millie, 15.*

Some girls are afraid their parents will react like Judy's. Judy is
sixteen.

*My parents were furious with me. Dad was so
angry. I thought he was going to hit me. Mom
just cried and cried. It was the worst night of
my life. It was worse than finding out I was
pregnant.*

Telling your parents you are pregnant may fill you with dread, so
before taking a look at some of the ways you might approach them,
let us say that some girls have legitimate reasons for not telling
parents. If this is the case with you, you will probably need to turn
to some other adult or agency to get the help you need. But if you
decide to tell your parents, ask yourself how they have reacted to
difficult situations in the past. Have there been occasions when you
have had to bring bad news? What did they say and do?

Many parents react negatively to bad news—anger, tears,
threats—but then once they recover from the shock, they do their
best to give the help that's needed. If this describes your parents,
they will probably react in much the same way to the news of your
pregnancy.

*I told my mom first. I just couldn't bear to tell
my father. He would be so disappointed in me.
My mom was really upset. She said Dad would
disown me, that he would kick me out of the
house. But after a few days, she calmed down
and helped me to tell Dad. They turned out to
be real understanding.—Bobbie, 17.*

You will have to wait out the storm, but, after it's over, your
parents may surprise you and show a depth of understanding you
never knew they had.

On the other hand, if bad news in the past has resulted in one or both parents becoming abusive or violent, it might not be safe to tell them without having another person with you. If you are having an abortion, it may not be necessary to tell them at all. However, if you are going to keep the baby, you will have to tell your parents sooner or later. Perhaps you can have a supportive adult accompany you or arrange to have your parents meet with you in a neutral setting such as a family planning clinic or a school counselor's office.

Some young women decide not to tell their parents because they don't want to cause them pain.

> *My mother doesn't need this. She and Dad just got divorced and she's having trouble finding a good job. This would just be too much. I don't want to hurt her any more than she has been already. If I can handle this by myself, it's better.—Ann, 17.*

Again, this is easier if you are having an abortion.

Many girls hesitate to tell their parents because they don't know what to say. It may be easier to talk to your mother first.

How do you begin? When is the best time? Choose a time when major tasks of the day like shopping, doctor's appointments, or work, are completed—when there is privacy and enough time to absorb the news of your pregnancy and discuss it.

When you have chosen a time, tell your mother you have something important to talk to her about. Once you have her attention, be direct and to the point. You might say, "I've had a pregnancy test and it came out positive." Or, "Maybe you've noticed that I've been feeling sick lately. Well, I think I'm pregnant." Better yet, you might simply say, "Mom, I'm pregnant."

If you feel too scared to tell your parents alone, bring your boyfriend with you, or your sister, a girlfriend, or an adult you have already confided in. If even that is more than you feel you can handle, ask one of them to tell your parents for you.

In addition, you might want to share this book, particularly this chapter, with your parents. It may help them to understand your situation and your feelings better as a result. This book can also serve as a basis for deciding together how to carry out your decision about your pregnancy.

Telling your parents may be the most painful and embarrassing experience you've ever had. They may be hearing for the first time something they didn't want to admit was possible—that their "child" is no longer a "child," but a sexually active young woman.

You may have discovered that since you became sexually active, your relationship to your parents has changed—that you don't want to share this part of your life with them. Being pregnant forces you to share it and to have to answer questions about it.

Telling them about it may make you very uncomfortable. They will want some facts. Some of the questions they are likely to ask are:

"Who is the boy?
"Is he the only one you've had sex with?"
"How long have you been having sex?"
"Why didn't you tell me you were having sex?"
"Why didn't you come to me so I could have helped you get birth control?"
"How long have you known you were pregnant?"
"Why didn't you tell me sooner?"

Answer them as honestly as you can. Tell them how you've handled your pregnancy so far. If you have decided what you plan to do, tell them your decision. If you are undecided and want their help, ask for it.

Sometimes, when parents find out their teenage daughter is pregnant, it stirs up feelings in them about themselves and their role as parents. They may feel they have failed somehow or that the pregnancy is a deliberate attempt to hurt them. This can cause them to say things in anger that may hurt you. In some parents, the anger never completely goes away. In most, after their feelings are spent, their love for you is obvious in the emotional support and practical help they provide.

Other parents do not view an unplanned pregnancy as a cause for anger or feelings of personal inadequacy. They view it as a crisis they may have to confront with a normal, healthy, teenage daughter who is traveling on the difficult road that carries her from childhood to adulthood.

One of the most positive outcomes of an unplanned pregnancy is that parents and daughter may begin talking to each other, maybe for the first time, about feelings and conflicts they have never shared before.

This experience in communicating holds the possibility of bringing you closer to your parents than you have ever been.

FIVE

MAKING ONE OF THE MOST IMPORTANT DECISIONS OF YOUR LIFE

When I found out I was pregnant, I felt very confused. I didn't know what to do. Abortion seemed wrong to me, but I didn't want to have a baby.—Joan, 16.

I felt happy to know that I was going to have a baby. It was nice to know that I could get pregnant. But, as time went by, I began to realize how much work a baby is. Now I'm not sure anymore that I should keep the baby. I'm thinking about adoption.—Dena, 15.

I was freaked out when I became pregnant. I mean, how could this happen to me? My boyfriend wanted me to keep the baby. My mother wanted me to have an abortion. I was stuck in the middle.—Carolyn, 18.

How to Begin Making this Important Decision

The pregnancy test is positive. You are pregnant. Many girls are shocked when they first learn the news. Some are happy. Others feel numb inside. Many cry. Your emotions may be overwhelming at first.

Now that you know for sure that you are pregnant, you must

decide what to do. The decision you make about the outcome of your pregnancy may be the most difficult one you have ever had to face. For most young women, it is a painful one, even if deep down inside they already know what they will do. It could be a decision that shapes the rest of your life.

Fortunately, there are choices. You can get married, you can raise the baby by yourself, you can agree to give up the baby for adoption, you can arrange for foster care, or you can have an abortion. Depending on your own unique circumstances, perhaps not all of these choices are open to you.

You may already have strong feelings about what you will decide. Many girls do.

> *I have a lot of goals to fulfill. I want to finish college and begin a career. Having a child right now will destroy every last one of them.— Trina, 19.*

> *There is no way I'd have an abortion. It's killing. I'm going to keep my baby. If my boyfriend will marry me, fine. If not, I'll raise the baby myself.—Blanca, 17.*

Many other girls are not sure what the best decision is for them. If you are undecided, read the chapter in this book that seems to be your first choice. Learn both the positive and negative aspects of that choice. Then take a look at the other chapters to find out what is involved in following a different direction. There might be an option there that seems right to you which you had not thought of before. As you read, take into account your own feelings, your personal values, your needs and your hopes for the future.

It's also helpful to write down your thoughts and feelings on paper. Make a list of the positive and negative things about each choice both for you and for the other significant people in your life. If you are feeling confused or undecided, making a list helps to clarify your thoughts and feelings.

Talking to someone you trust often helps. However, as you discuss your options with others—whether it be your boyfriend, your parents, or a counselor—remember, you are the person who will have to take responsibility for and live with the consequences of your decision.

Your decision will affect other people, but in the end, it will affect you most. Make your decision carefully and thoughtfully. It could change the direction of your life.

The First Choice

The first choice you must make is whether you should continue your pregnancy or end it by having an abortion. Time becomes very important in this decision. If you do not want a child right now, it's in your own best interest to get an abortion in the first trimester—that is, the first three months of pregnancy, or twelve weeks from the first day of your last normal period. It's safer, simpler, and less expensive. Too often, time and the biological process make the decision for a pregnant teenager.

> When I telephoned the clinic and they told me I was pregnant, I hung up on them. I didn't want to hear it. I was so afraid. I didn't tell anybody for months. Finally, my gym teacher called me in and asked if I was pregnant. She was the first person I told. By then it was way too late for me to get an abortion. So, I have to have the baby.—Mary, 15.

Even though Mary must have her baby now, she can still decide whether to give the child up for adoption, place it temporarily in a foster home, or raise it herself.

An unexpected pregnancy has the effect of making you feel you have lost control, not only over your own body, but over your life. One way to regain control is to focus on the process of weighing your alternatives until a decision is reached.

Continuing the Pregnancy

Teenagers faced with an unplanned pregnancy react in different ways. Some make the decision to keep their babies after mature consideration. They love children, feel they are ready to be mothers, and expect to enjoy taking care of a baby.

Others feel that it gives them leverage in their relationship with a boyfriend and/or parents. Because they are pregnant, their needs cannot be ignored or dismissed. They must be taken seriously.

Yet others feel the baby is the only "friend" they have. They expect the baby to relieve their feelings of loneliness and provide them with the love they feel is missing in their lives.

Some continue their pregnancy because they feel abortion is wrong.

Still other teens become mothers "by accident." They postpone making a decision until it is too late. Time makes the decision for them. By doing nothing at all, you are deciding to have a baby.

No matter how your choice is made, there are many important things to consider. If you are still in the first three months of pregnancy, the knowledge that you are carrying a fetus inside of you may not seem real. You may have no outward signs of pregnancy at all. You know you are pregnant, but the idea of having a baby is still just that—an idea.

The actual realization that you are going to become a mother usually begins when you start to feel movement. This happens between the sixteenth and the twenty-second weeks of pregnancy.

Before this happens, it's necessary to prepare for all the changes that will occur in your life so that you can make plans for coping with them.

A good way to begin is by asking yourself some questions:

—Why do I want a baby?
—Do I feel old enough to become a mother?
—How will having a baby change my life now and in the future?
—How will having a baby change my relationship with my

boyfriend/mother/father/other important people in my life?

—How will I pay the doctor and hospital for my prenatal and delivery care?

—If I cannot depend on help from my boyfriend or parents, how will I pay for food/clothing/and a place to live for myself and my baby?

—Will I be able to meet the feeding, bathing, diapering, and laundry demands of a baby 24 hours a day?

—Will I be able to care for a sick or irritable baby?

—Will I have enough energy to care for my baby and still go to school or work?

—If so, who will care for my baby during the hours I am away?

—How do I see myself, my child, and my life one year from now?

Having a baby is exciting and brings pleasure and fun. Always being on call with a baby who depends on you for everything can also be exhausting and irritating. Even the most loving parents sometimes feel trapped.

Babies may seem like dolls, but they are real human beings, incapable of surviving alone. In addition to food, shelter, and clothing, they require a lot of holding, touching, and talking to—in other words, a lot of love and caring—in order to develop normally and feel safe in a world they can trust. Even the way a baby is picked up, put down, held and handled, influences how she/he will view the world as she/he grows up.

It's important to find out how you can provide the basics for your child. Don't assume someone else will provide them. Carey, 16, counted on her girlfriend to help.

> *Before I had my baby, my best friend promised she'd always be there to help me and the baby. But after the baby was born, she got tired of coming around to visit me. She went back to her friends and having fun.*

Your parents may want to help, but sooner or later you will want to become independent of them. Sharon, 19, tells of her experience.

I was away at school when I became pregnant. I felt very happy about it. Very grown up. I was a woman now, I thought. Then I had my kid and I had to move back into my parents' house because I didn't have any money. I don't like living in my old bedroom with the baby's crib stuck in there. I'm home all day long. I can't find a job. I have to ask my parents for every dollar I spend. I wish I could go back to college, but the baby takes up all the money my family can afford.

Find out for sure how you will manage. Be realistic. Can those who promise to help be depended upon? If not, can you carry the responsibility alone?

If you are going to have a baby, you will need proper medical care. That means you should see an obstetrician—a doctor who specializes in pregnant women, childbirth, and just-born infants—at least once a month during your pregnancy.

Deciding to carry a baby within your body means your responsibility to it has already begun. You need to take especially good care of yourself by eating healthy foods, getting enough rest, and taking vitamins your doctor recommends. Also you should *stop* smoking cigarettes, drinking alcohol, and taking drugs. Everything you take into your body goes into your baby's body. Your baby's health is directly affected by the care you give it before it is born.

If you are thinking about continuing your pregnancy, read Chapter 11 on caring for yourself and your baby during your pregnancy.

Giving birth is a very important event in your life. Whether you decide to get married, raise the child yourself, or opt for adoption or foster care, you will want to make the best decision for your baby and for yourself.

Ending the Pregnancy

Many girls and women who have unplanned pregnancies feel that abortion is the best decision for them. Many young women do not feel ready for parenthood.

> *I was only recently engaged to my boyfriend when I found out I was pregnant. I guess I could have married him right away, but we decided being parents isn't what we wanted for the first year of our marriage. Besides, we can't afford it and with both of us working, there is no time for a baby.—Karen, 19.*

In fact, the reason most girls decide to have abortions is because they feel they are not ready to be mothers, they don't have enough money to raise a child, and they have education or career goals to attain first.

Some teenagers, however, are made to feel that they *must* have an abortion either by their boyfriends or by their parents.

> *My boyfriend told me to get rid of it. So I had an abortion which is what he wanted.—Terri, 18.*

> *My mom and dad said they didn't want any-body to know that I got pregnant. I wanted to keep the baby, but they took me to get an abortion.—Diedra, 14.*

Just as no one should force you to continue your pregnancy, no one should force you to end your pregnancy. Having an abortion is as serious a decision to make as having a baby. It is never an easy choice to make, but it ultimately should be *your* choice.

Some people have religious beliefs about abortion that makes this choice a difficult one to accept. Sheri, 16, was one of them.

> *I had been taught that abortion is a sin, but I think bringing a baby in this world that you*

*don't want is even a bigger sin. It was a hard
choice, but I believe I made the right one by
having an abortion.*

If you are thinking about having an abortion, you should make arrangements for one as soon as possible. As we talked about before, the earlier you have an abortion, the better it is for you. A first trimester abortion (done in the first twelve weeks of pregnancy) is safer, simpler, and less expensive than a second trimester abortion (which is done between the thirteenth and twenty-fourth weeks of pregnancy). A later abortion is more difficult, has greater risks, and costs more. In addition, many states have regulations that can prevent a woman from getting an abortion after the first twelve weeks. After twenty-four weeks, you will not be able to get an abortion at all and you will have to give birth to the baby.

A first trimester abortion is safer than childbirth, especially for a teenager. A legal abortion performed by a medical doctor will not affect your ability to have children in the future. To learn more about what an abortion is and how other teenagers coped with their decision, read Chapter 6.

Abortion is a very personal decision. Only *you* can decide if this is the right choice for you.

Making the Decision that Will Affect the Rest of Your Life

Making an important decision is never easy, especially when you are pressured by time. Let's review the five steps for making a decision that's right for you, a decision you can live with.

1) *Learn what your choices are.*
   You have already begun to do this by reading this book. The next few chapters will tell you more about abortion, marriage, adoption, foster care, and raising a child alone.

Read other books as well. Talk to counselors, family, and friends. Learn all that you can.

2) *Figure out the positive and negative aspects of each choice.* Think about what each choice means to you. Make a list of the positive and negative aspects of each choice you are considering. You may waver back and forth between two or more choices. This is normal when faced with a difficult decision. "Try on" your choices. See which one "fits" you best.

3) *Choose one.*

Once you have learned what your choices are and you have thought carefully about them, one choice will emerge as being the right one for you. Review the reasons why this is the best decision for you. If the reasons are still strong and make good sense to you, the decision making process is completed.

4) *Act on your choice.*

Put your decision into action by making a telephone call, talking with the appropriate person, or by going to the place that can help you to fulfill your decision. Keep moving forward.

5) *Accept the positives and negatives of your choice.*

In order to live comfortably with your decision, recognize that you may continue to have mixed feelings about it. Remember you made your choice for reasons that were valid for you. If there are still negative feelings about your choice, tell someone who will listen. Talking about them helps to take them into yourself and accept them. Also, try to keep in mind the good things about your decision. Remember *why* you made the choice you did.

By learning about your options, talking to others, and exploring your own feelings, you will be in a better position to make a decision about the outcome of your pregnancy—a decision you can live with.

SIX

ABORTION

I always thought if I ever did get pregnant, I'd have the baby. But when I actually was pregnant, I decided to have an abortion. I have no money and no husband. I didn't want to end up a single mother on welfare.—Corrie, 16.

I feel guilty about having an abortion, but I'm only fifteen. I want to finish high school and be with my friends. I don't have any money. You know, what could I do for this kid?—Nanci, 15.

I felt so relieved after my abortion. It was great not being pregnant anymore. I have been so bogged down for weeks by this thing and now I can get back to my normal life again.—Bettie, 19.

Deciding for Abortion

Most single teenage girls who become pregnant decide to terminate their pregnancies by having an abortion. The decision is usually reached after much thought and weighing of alternatives. It may be complicated by feelings about their own sexuality, their relationship to their boyfriend and parents, their religious upbringing, and the meaning pregnancy and abortion holds for each of them.

There may be a part of you that wants to have a baby and another part that shudders at the thought. Sometimes, these two opposite wishes seem to be at battle within you, leaving you feeling that you can't make any decision at all. The choice should be made after realistically considering which alternative you feel you can cope with best.

If you are considering abortion, you may be having one or all of these feelings. Try to sort them out. Talk about them with another person. Most importantly, *feel* them! By doing so, you begin to deal with them. Mixed feelings are to be expected. Expressing them helps you to accept them and the abortion.

> *I wish I didn't have to have an abortion. I wish I hadn't gotten pregnant. But now that I am, I think it's better for me to have an abortion than to have a child that I don't want.—Lorayne, 16.*

The young women who decide to have an abortion do so for many reasons.

- They feel too young to have a baby.
- They don't have enough money to raise a child.
- They don't have a stable relationship with their sexual partner.
- They want to finish high school/go to college/have a career.
- They want to be married before starting a family.

The law in the United States today that permits abortion is based on a woman's right to privacy, her right to control her own body, and her right to decide whether she will have children and when. It gives you the choice to have a legal and medically safe abortion. It's up to you to decide if abortion is the right choice for you.

Questions About Abortion

There are lots of myths about abortions. The two major ones are:

—abortion causes damage to reproductive organs making it impossible to have future children.
—abortion causes death.

Perhaps you have heard such stories from friends or older relatives. Many of these stories come from a time when abortions were illegal in this country. They were then performed in secret, often by people who were not physicians. Many women attempted to perform abortions on themselves. Sometimes the instruments used were not the right ones and not sterile. If there were complications, the woman often received no help.

This is not the case today. Abortion is a medically safe and simple procedure performed by licensed physicians in an appropriate medical setting.

Up to sixteen weeks of pregnancy, abortion is safer than any other outcome of pregnancy. This means that the risk of dying from abortion is seven times lower than it is for childbirth. Up to twelve weeks of pregnancy, an abortion carries the same risk as a shot of penicillin. Women are closely followed by the doctors who perform the abortion. If a complication should occur, the woman is immediately treated.

Let's take a look at the questions most asked by teenage girls.

How many abortions can I have?
Repeated abortions, with repeated dilation (stretching) of the cervix, may lead to cervical incompetence. This is a condition that can cause problems for the woman who wants to carry a future pregnancy to term, because the cervix may stretch before the nine months of pregnancy are completed, resulting in miscarriage or premature birth. This appears to be more likely if abortions are performed late in the pregnancy or within several months of each other. There is no agreement on how many abortions a woman can have before this becomes a factor.

How big is the embryo or the fetus?
The fertilized egg quickly divides and multiplies. After three weeks, this cluster of cells becomes an embryo. In eight weeks it is approximately one inch in size. After the eighth week it is called a fetus. At twelve weeks of pregnancy, the fetus is about three inches long.

Do my parents have to know?

Most clinics will perform a first trimester abortion without inform-ing your parents. (But be sure to ask what the policy is beforehand.) Almost every hospital, though, will require parental consent for an abortion involving a young teenager. Hospital policies vary. Some require consent if you are under 18, some if you are under 16. Find out the policy in your hospital. Since second trimester abortions are almost always performed in a hospital and frequently involve an overnight stay, parental permission is needed.

When can I get an abortion?

You can get a first trimester abortion up to twelve weeks of your pregnancy. This is the simplest and safest abortion. It can be done in a clinic and is available in every state. A second trimester abortion can be performed between the thirteenth and twenty-fourth week of pregnancy. This abortion is usually done in a hospital and is restricted in many states. After twenty-four weeks, a legal abortion cannot be performed except in the extreme circum-stance when the physical health of the mother is in danger.

How much does an abortion cost?

First trimester abortions done in a clinic can cost anywhere from $150 to $300. Second trimester abortions are more costly. Most clinics and hospitals want to be paid on the day of the abortion in cash or with a money order, a certified check, or traveler's checks. Ask what the policy is in the clinic you choose.

How long does the actual abortion take?

A first trimester vacuum aspiration (suction) abortion takes approximately two to seven minutes to perform. The amount of time spent in a clinic or a hospital from check-in to recovery is usually between four and six hours.

Will it hurt?

If general anesthesia is used, the actual abortion will not hurt at all since you are asleep. When you wake up, you will feel cramps which may last for several hours. There will be drowsiness and a heavy feeling along with possible nausea, which are the aftereffects of the general anesthesia. If local anesthesia is used, there may be pain during the actual abortion; however, it lasts for only a few minutes. Cramping will continue for several hours. There are little or no aftereffects related to local anesthesia.

Will I be able to have children after an abortion?
Yes. Abortion does not affect your ability to conceive. In fact, some girls become pregnant before their next period returns. This is why it is important to talk to your counselor about using a good birth control method.

Will anyone be able to tell I've had an abortion?
No. Not even a gynecologist can tell you've had a first trimester abortion. Because of this, it is important that you let a gynecologist know you've had an abortion at the time when you decide to have a child or if you have a second abortion, so that he or she can provide you with appropriate health care.

Isn't there some other way I can end a pregnancy?
No. There is nothing you can drink, eat, or swallow that will end your pregnancy. You may have heard about certain methods or substances to take to bring on your period. They won't work and they might be poisonous. Falling down stairs, vigorous exercise, or punching your stomach will not work either. *Never* attempt to insert anything, such as a knitting needle or a coat hanger, into your uterus. You can perforate (put a hole in) your uterus, cause infection, or massive bleeding. Permanent damage or death could follow.

An abortion is a medical procedure and should be done only by a trained and licensed physician. Abortions are now legal. They are the safest medical procedures being done today. You have the right and the responsibility to decide for a safe, legal abortion.

How And Where to Get an Abortion

The best place for a young woman to have a first trimester abortion is in a state licensed clinic which specializes in abortion and has skilled physicians. A good clinic will have an experienced staff who can deal with all aspects of abortion. In addition, state licensed clinics provide counseling, whereas private doctors and hospitals usually do not.

To find out where to get an abortion, check your local newspaper advertisement section or the Yellow Pages under "Abortion," "Birth Control," "Clinics," "Family Planning," and "Health Agencies." Any Planned Parenthood office will also be able to help you. Check the State-by-State listings at the back of this book.

Make a telephone call to the clinic or, if you can get there easily, make a visit. You'll get an idea from that first phone call or visit how friendly and welcoming they are. Do they take time to answer your questions and offer information?

Some important questions to ask are:

- Does the clinic have board certified or board eligible obstetrical-gynecological (OB-GYN) physicians?
- Do they have hospital backup? Which hospital? How far is it?
- Is there a 24-hour hot line service in case there is a complication?
- Is counseling available?
- Do they have a laboratory on the premises?

If the clinic you are calling does not have all these qualifications, you may want to look for another one that does. Remember—feel free to ask questions. You have the right to receive the information you need in order to get the best health care possible.

In addition, you may want to ask:

- Will you need your parents' consent?
- Will your parents be notified?

- What kind of anesthesia is offered?
- How much will the entire abortion cost?
- How much will the followup examination cost?
- Will you be able to talk to a counselor alone?
- Can you bring a friend, your boyfriend, your mother?
- Can your companion be with you during the procedure?

An abortion can seem expensive, especially to a teenager (but less expensive than childbirth). If you don't have the money, you will have to find ways to get the amount needed.

- Can you tell your parents about ending your pregnancy? They might be able to help you pay for the abortion. Their medical insurance may cover part or all of the cost of the abortion.
- Ask your partner if he can help. Maybe he can borrow the money from a friend or a relative. Can his parents help out? If he has a job, perhaps he can get an advance in salary.
- Borrow small amounts of money from a lot of different friends. If you would rather not tell them it's for an abortion, say it's for a personal emergency.
- If you have a job, ask for an advance in salary.
- Take out whatever savings you have.
- Combine the above suggestions to come up with the money you need.

If you still cannot get enough money together, tell the clinic about your situation. Tell them how much money you do have. They might be able to arrange for a deferred payment or a reduced fee. You might be referred to a social agency for assistance.

Don't be embarrassed to talk about money. Most clinics have a policy for accommodating teenagers. Don't let the lack of money keep you from calling a clinic and making inquiries. The longer you wait, the more expensive an abortion will be.

Almost every state has some kind of abortion facility, but in some areas these clinics may be far away from where you live. Call an abortion hot line or the nearest hospital. Someone there will be able to link you up with an abortion service.

You might consider talking to your parents. If you have as much information as possible before telling them, you can help them to understand your situation better. Be able to tell them where the clinic is, when you can have an appointment for an abortion, and how much it will cost. In addition, if you have talked to a counselor, a minister, or a health care person, your parents may be reassured and will probably see that you are capable of making a difficult decision and carrying it out maturely. Most parents turn out to be far more helpful than teenagers expect them to be.

First Trimester Abortion

A first trimester abortion is called a suction or vacuum aspiration procedure. It is the most common method used to end a pregnancy. It can be done in an out-patient clinic (no overnight stay) and is performed up to twelve weeks of pregnancy.

Since the admission process takes time, there may be some periods of waiting on the day of your abortion. It might be a good idea to bring along a book, a magazine, or some needlework to pass the time. You may also want to bring your boyfriend, your mother, or a friend.

When you arrive at the clinic, a medical chart is prepared for you and you are admitted. Admission includes taking a medical history, a urine sample to test for pregnancy, and a blood sample to test for blood type. (About one in ten people have Rh-negative blood. This is not unusual. It means they lack a substance found in red blood cells called the Rh factor. If a woman has Rh-negative blood and carries a fetus with Rh-positive blood, antibodies from the mother's body destroy the Rh-positive blood cells in the fetus. An injection of Rhogam following an abortion protects the fetus in a future pregnancy.)

A good clinic will offer individual or group counseling before the abortion procedure. The counselor explains the procedure and answers your questions. She can also help you with your feelings and concerns about your pregnancy and your abortion decision. Birth control is also discussed. Most women find that the counseling session is a very positive and supportive experience.

> *I knew I wanted an abortion, but I wasn't sure my reasons for wanting one were good enough. After talking with my counselor, I felt much better and much more confident that I was making the right choice for me.—Charlene, 17.*

After you are changed into a hospital gown and your blood pressure is taken, you will lie down on an examining table with your legs elevated in stirrups while the doctor performs an internal pelvic examination to determine the size of your uterus. By doing this, the doctor can judge how pregnant you are. This final estimation is always done by the physician performing the abortion. The abortion procedure follows this examination.

General anesthesia is usually given intravenously by inserting a small needle in your arm. You will fall asleep almost immediately and will feel nothing during the actual abortion. A short time later, you wake up in the recovery room. The abortion is completed. You can expect to feel cramps and a sense of heavy-headedness, dizziness, or nausea, until the general anesthesia completely wears off. You will be given something to eat and drink while you rest. When you have recovered from the effects of the procedure, you are given aftercare instructions and are discharged.

If you are having local anesthesia, you may be given a mild tranquilizer to relax you first. The doctor then injects a novocaine-like anesthetic onto or near the cervix to numb it. This feels like a pinch and lasts only a few seconds.

The cervix is then dilated (stretched) by a long cylindrical instrument called a dilator. After the dilation is completed, a sterile tube called a cannula is inserted through the opening of the cervix into the uterus. The cannula is attached to the suctioning machine.

The doctor gently moves the cannula around the inside of the uterus removing the fetal tissue and uterine lining.

There may be some pain during the procedure, but it will not last for long. Try to breathe in and out in a slow rhythmic pattern. Hold the hand of a nurse, counselor, or your companion.

When it is over, there will probably be some cramping. You will be escorted to the recovery room where you will receive nourishment and rest until you receive aftercare instructions and are discharged.

You are no longer pregnant.

> *What a feeling of relief. I felt as if this enormous burden were lifted off my shoulders. I didn't even care about the pain. I just felt great.—Dawn, 16.*

Second Trimester Abortion

Between the twelfth and fourteenth week of pregnancy, a Dilation and Curettage (D & C) abortion can be performed. If you are under the age limit at your particular hospital (which might be 16, 17, or 18), parental consent will be needed. A D & C abortion is often done in a hospital. General anesthesia is usually used. The actual abortion takes about ten to twenty minutes. It can cost between $300 and $400. Some physicians are skilled in performing this procedure beyond fourteen weeks. The fee rises accordingly.

This type of abortion is similar to the suction abortion; however, the cervix must be opened more because the pregnancy is more advanced. Dilation may be achieved either by the use of a dilator or by insertion of laminaria (small "sticks" of sterile, dried seaweed). Instead of the cannula, a curette (a long handled spoon-shaped instrument) is used to empty the uterus. Sometimes the cannula is alternated with the curette to remove the contents of the uterus. This abortion is properly called Dilation and Evacuation (D & E).

Occasionally, an overnight stay in the hospital may be necessary, though most often you can return home the same day. The cramping from the abortion, and the drowsy, nauseous feeling from the general anesthetic, will be about the same as for a first trimester abortion. You should follow the same instructions for the aftercare.

Between sixteen and twenty-four weeks, a saline (salt solution) or a prostaglandin (synthetic hormone) abortion can be performed. This is also called an induced abortion because it is really a medically induced miscarriage. It is always done in a hospital and, again, requires parental consent if you are under 16, 17, or 18, depending on hospital policy. You will have to stay overnight and possibly up to three nights. It can cost between $350 and $600.

After changing into a hospital gown, this procedure is performed by injecting a local anesthetic just below the navel. Then a hollow needle is inserted through the abdominal wall into the uterus. Some of the amniotic fluid which surrounds the fetus is withdrawn through the needle and the fluid is replaced with a saline or prostaglandin solution. (Sometimes, prostaglandin is given intravenously.) Most women experience some abdominal pressure during this procedure. After the needle is removed, a Band-Aid is placed over the needlemark. Most hospitals give pitocin (another synthetic hormone) to start contractions of the uterus.

Contractions increase until the fetus and placenta are expelled through the vagina. Contractions are felt as cramps. Medication is given for pain during this process which takes between twelve and seventy-two hours. The average time is twenty-four to thirty-six hours.

When it is over, you will be given aftercare instructions and you will be discharged.

Physical Aftercare

Most teenagers recover rapidly from an abortion, with little or no physical aftereffects. After a good night's sleep, they feel back to normal. Following either a first or a second trimester abortion, you will be given instructions for aftercare and a followup examination.

After the abortion there will be vaginal bleeding for anywhere from one day to two or three weeks. This is not your menstrual period. The bleeding should be light to moderate and may be on-and-off for several days. Sometimes you might pass small blood clots, which is normal. Mild cramps may continue for a day or two. Your menstrual period returns in about four to six weeks, but can take up to two months. If it does not begin by then, contact your doctor.

You are expected to have a followup examination in two to three weeks, depending on whether you had a first or second trimester abortion. Follow the instructions given by your physician.

From the time of your abortion until you have had your follow-up exam, nothing must enter your vagina. This means no vaginal intercourse. No tampons. No douching. No fingers. In addition, no tub baths (you can take showers) and no swimming. Your cervix has been dilated and it takes time for it to return to normal. Therefore, anything that goes into your vagina could allow bacteria to travel through your open cervix and into your uterus, and possibly cause infection.

In addition, avoid strenuous activities such as jogging, vigorous dancing, horseback riding, playing tennis, or lifting heavy objects. You can resume these activities after seeing your doctor.

Complications sometimes occur before your followup examination. This happens about once per one hundred first trimester abortion procedures. The two most common complications are infection and incomplete abortion. Both can be treated. There are some signs to watch for. If you experience any of them, call your clinic, hospital, or doctor *immediately.*

- Excessive bleeding (saturating 2 sanitary napkins in one hour).
- The passing of large blood clots (the size of a half-dollar).
- Excessive cramping that is not relieved by Tylenol.
- A fever of 100 degrees or more.
- An unusual or foul smelling vaginal discharge.

The chances for a complication are small, but it can happen. Pay attention to how you are feeling. Even if you only suspect something is wrong, or need more information about what you are experiencing, call the clinic or your doctor. They want to help you get the best physical aftercare possible.

In general, it's good to get plenty of rest, eat right, and take it easy until your body has completely recovered.

Emotional After Care

The most common feeling following an abortion is one of relief. The days and weeks of dealing with a crisis are over. The decision has been made and carried out. Contrary to the myth that abortion causes mental problems, most young women integrate the experience, move on with their lives, and have no serious long-term effects.

Following the abortion, there may be crying that you don't understand.

> *When I woke up from the anesthetic and I realized the abortion was over, I sobbed uncontrollably for the longest time. But after a while, it passed, and I began to feel better.—Karen, 18.*

This is often a side effect of general anesthesia and may also be a release of the tension you felt before the procedure. It is often an expression of grieving and sadness for the loss of the fetus. It is a mourning process and a healthy sign that you are not blocking out your feelings. Expressing them, sharing them with someone, relieves you of the pain they bring and helps you regain control of them.

Sometimes, for a week or two, there is a short period of depression—a feeling of letdown as the intensity of the experience lessens. It's similar to the "postpartum blues" women sometimes feel after childbirth.

Part of the reason for this is biological. Because your body is changing from a pregnant state to a nonpregnant state, your hormones get out of balance for a while until your menstrual cycle is regulated again. You may notice some body changes due to this, such as your abdomen getting flatter, and your breasts returning to normal size and becoming less tender.

When the decision for abortion has been the choice of the young woman herself, and she was sure it was the right choice for her, there is little or no emotional aftermath.

If the decision was not hers, but that of someone important in her life—her boyfriend or parents—there may be feelings of anger, hurt, and resentment. She may feel they have deprived her of something very precious, and that they don't care about her feelings. If they left the decision up to her but refused to help her, leaving her unable to continue her pregnancy alone, she may feel abandoned. If she has not told anyone, she may feel isolated from others by carrying so heavy a secret by herself. If she has strong moral or religious objections to abortion, she may feel overwhelmed by guilt.

Feelings of anger, deprivation, and guilt have more to do with how you feel about your relationship to your boyfriend and parents, and how you feel about yourself and your life situation, than to the abortion itself. If you begin to deal with them, you can begin to deal with the abortion.

It may help to speak to a counselor. Sometimes it only takes one or two meetings to gain some understanding of your feelings. If it takes longer, the counselor can refer you to someone you can see on a weekly basis for a while.

Making difficult choices helps you to know yourself better. Carrying them out gives you confidence in your ability to deal with a crisis.

SEVEN

MARRIAGE

I got married when I was six months pregnant. My parents weren't too happy about it, but they gave us a real nice wedding. Jimmy and I are very much in love. The baby made us get married sooner than we would have ordinarily, that's all.—Kim, 18.

I really loved Tommy, but I guess we weren't ready for marriage. He wanted to play football with the other guys while I was stuck at home looking after our baby. I guess we felt our lives were being stifled. It was too much to handle and we ended up getting divorced.—Lisa, 16.

Next to getting pregnant, getting married was the dumbest thing I did. We fought all the time. Finally, he took off, and that was the end of our marriage.—Cathy, 17.

Teenage Marriage

Most young people today have had sexual experience by the time they get married. But an unexpected pregnancy is one of the major reasons why teenagers decide to get married.

The decision for marriage, like the decision to keep your baby, is one of the most important choices you'll have to make in your life.

Because it is a difficult choice and one that is not open to everybody, only about 10 percent of pregnant teenage girls marry before the baby is born.

A young couple will be faced with many difficulties when they decide to be married. Many teenagers get married before they really know themselves or what they want out of life. The responsibilities of being self-supporting, making a marriage work, and raising a baby are often a great deal to take on all at once. Since keeping the baby is a decision you must make along with your decision to marry, it may be helpful to read Chapters 10 and 11 to learn more about what it means to carry a child to term and begin to raise it.

Many people bring expectations to the marriage which can't be fulfilled. For these and many other reasons, teenage parents have much higher divorce rates than couples who have children in later years. Some studies show that more than half of school-age parents split up within five years.

The statistics may look grim, but some young marriages do survive. If you are thinking about marriage, discuss it with your parents. It's a good idea to get together with your boyfriend and his parents or have a meeting with both sets of parents. Talk to other people you might know who got married when they were your age. Try speaking to a counselor or a clergyman. They may be able to help you sort out your feelings about marriage.

In the end, of course, only you can decide if you want to marry the boy who got you pregnant. You are the one who will have to live with him on a day-to-day basis. Is he the person you want to share the rest of your life with?

Teenage marriages that survive do so most often when the young man and woman are deeply committed to each other and are determined to make their marriage work. There may be problems, but many teenagers have shown that they can adjust to, and even overcome, the difficulties of an early marriage due to an unplanned pregnancy.

Who Can Get Married?

Because marriage is a serious step, each state has particular legal requirements. If you are over 18, or are an emancipated minor (that is, you live by yourself and support yourself financially), you have the right to be married in almost every state without parental consent. If you are under 18, you will most likely need your parents' permission to marry. In some states, the age of consent might be higher or lower. Some teenagers travel to another state where the age of consent is lower so that they can marry without their parents' permission.

To learn about the law in your state, telephone the "Marriage License Bureau" in your town, city, or county, or consult your rabbi, priest, or minister.

In addition, each state has different laws concerning the waiting period for getting a marriage license. Premarital blood tests must also be taken in most states, and there is a time limitation on how long the test is valid. A blood test is taken to make sure that neither you nor your partner has venereal disease. This is for the protection of your unborn child to whom V.D. can be transmitted.

There is a charge for the blood tests and for the marriage license. Fees vary from state to state and from year to year. Call a doctor or clinic, or the Marriage License Bureau, for more information.

If you are planning to be married in a church or synagogue, you will want to make arrangements with your clergyman or rabbi. He or she may want to talk to you and your intended husband before you are married. Some religious organizations offer premarital counseling. It's a good idea to participate in any counseling available, because it is an opportunity to talk about subjects that are important in establishing a solid marriage.

Since many churches and synagogues celebrate several weddings each month and are especially booked in May, June, and December, you will want to set the date and time for your wedding as soon as possible. If you are planning to wear a traditional wedding gown, it might be helpful to know that most women do not look obviously pregnant until the fourth month. After that, you may be limited in selecting a dress style, or you may have to choose a maternity bridal outfit.

You should also begin planning the details of your ceremony and discussing them with your future husband, your clergyman and your parents.

> *When I got pregnant, keeping the baby and getting married seemed like the natural thing to do. My boyfriend is in the Navy, so we had a real military-style wedding in my church. My husband looked so handsome in his uniform, and even though I was three months pregnant, I wore a veil and a long white dress. After the ceremony, we left the church through the traditional arch of crossed swords. It was beautiful.*
> *—Debbie, 16.*

"Is Marriage For Me?"

When thinking about getting married, begin by understanding that marriage signifies a major change in your life. It means establishing an intimate, permanent bond with another human being. Your position in society will be altered. The relationship you have with your parents and with your friends will also be changed. And, you will soon become a mother with new responsibilities. You will begin to form a close relationship with yet another human being—your baby.

Before you decide for marriage, it's a good idea to ask yourself and your potential husband questions.

The most important question you should ask is "*Why* do I want to get married?" This is a very serious question. Try to answer it for yourself as honestly as you can.

Do you want to marry because you feel you should now that you are pregnant? Are you being pushed into marriage by your boyfriend or your parents? Do you feel guilty about having had sex and want to get married in order to feel better about being sexually active? Do you want to prove that you will be a better wife and mother than your own mother? Do you want to be taken care of?

Or, do you want to marry because you are deeply in love with your boyfriend and are committed to him and to making your marriage work? Are you looking forward to sharing the rest of your life with him? Are you prepared to take on the responsibility and the joy of parenthood with the young man you hope to marry?

> *Stan and I have been going together since ninth grade. We had an understanding we would be married someday. When I got pregnant, we discussed abortion, but then decided we would both be much happier if we got married and started our family now.—Rita, 18.*

Ask your boyfriend why *he* wants to get married. Does he feel he has to? Does he get nervous or angry when you talk about marriage? Does he feel bad about getting you pregnant and, by marrying you, hopes to make you and himself feel better? Does he feel it's his "duty," that marriage is the "right" thing to do under the circumstances? Is he being pressured by his parents or by your mom and dad to marry you now that you are pregnant?

Without a strong sense of love and commitment to you and the baby when it comes, marriage will probably prove to be a difficult decision to live with for both of you.

One of the major reasons why a pregnant teenager might want to get married is to "legitimize this child" or to "give the baby a name." You may be worried about what people will think of you if you don't get married. You might also be concerned that your child will suffer in the future for having been born to an unmarried mother. These are substantial concerns. Some girls decide to marry for these reasons, even though they realize the marriage will probably end in divorce.

Only you can weigh the seriousness of your decision. If you do divorce, you may still have to explain to your child why you had to get married in the first place.

It might be helpful to know that your own last name is sufficient for any birth certificate. Or if you wish, you can give your child any last name you choose.

Some girls want to get married because they no longer want to live at home or because they are hoping that a husband will fulfill their needs. Unfortunately, most girls who marry in order to "get" something will be disappointed. More often than not, marriage means giving and sharing.

If you and your boyfriend have a long-standing relationship and feel that you do love each other, you still should explore some of the important practical aspects of marriage before making a final decision.

Take a look at the following questions with your boyfriend and talk over your answers together.

What do you expect to give to your marriage?

- What do you expect from him?
- What does your future husband expect to give to the marriage?
- What does he expect from you?

What are your goals?

- Do you have any career goals?
- Do you want to be able to stay home and raise several children?
- Do you plan to continue your education?
- What does your intended husband see as his job/career goals?
- Where do you want to live someday?
- What kind of a lifestyle do you want?
- What do each of you hope to accomplish in your lives?

Who is going to make what decisions in your family?

- Do you want to make the decisions about some areas and your boyfriend in others?
- Do you plan to discuss major issues and decide jointly?
- What about the day-to-day decisions?

- How will you decide matters concerning your child?

Where are you going to live?
- Do you both plan to stay in the same city or town?
- Have you begun looking for an apartment or a house?
- Can you afford it?
- Is it possible or desirable to live with either set of parents until you are more financially secure?

How are you going to divide up money?
- Can you find a job or continue working after the baby is born?
- How will you share the bills and everyday household expenses?
- If only your husband earns a salary, how much of that will go to your baby, your home, you?

How will you share caring for the baby and doing the household chores?
- Does he expect you to do all the cooking, cleaning and washing?
- In what ways can he share in some of these tasks?
- Is he willing to help feed the baby, diaper the baby, get up in the middle of the night to care for the baby?

These might seem like very nitty-gritty subjects to be talking about, and sometimes it's painful to discuss them, especially when there are disagreements. You will undoubtedly have differences. That's natural. No two people can agree on everything. What is important is to be able to discuss these issues *beforehand* and try to come to terms with each other's expectations.

If you both can talk openly about these questions, understand what you can expect from one another, and are able to make adjustments and compromises, you are probably on the right track to a successful marriage relationship.

Why Do So Many Marriages Go Wrong?

The divorce rate for teenagers is high. In fact, the younger the couple who gets married, the greater the chance for divorce. Not every teenage marriage fails, but it's worthwhile to take a look at some of the major reasons why so many do. By understanding what the problems are, you may want to think more carefully about marrying, or you might find that you will be able to overcome the difficulties when you face them.

Probably the single greatest reason why marriages fail is *unfulfilled expectations.* We all have hopes and dreams of what marriage will be like and what it will do for us. Many times, though, what we want cannot be had through marriage alone.

These misexpectations can take many forms.

Often a girl *wants to be taken care of* by her husband, particularly when she is going to have a baby. It's a vulnerable time for women of any age and a time when they feel more strongly their dependency on others. A young woman may feel frightened of taking on the responsibility for a baby, and so she marries with the expectation that her husband will take care of both of them.

Sometimes a girl will marry because she *wishes to be independent of her mother and father.* She may see her parents as being overly strict or feel that she doesn't have the freedom to do as she pleases. In some cases, she may have had to endure family problems such as parental alcoholism, drug abuse, or violence. For whatever reason, she wants to escape from her parents' home. Getting married seems like the quickest and easiest way out. Too often, though, a young woman will find that her husband's home is just as oppressive as her parents'. He may have his own demands and rules. When the baby comes, a girl can find herself doubly trapped.

Another reason why a teenager may want to get married is to "automatically" *become an adult.* In our society, marriage and motherhood certainly seem to mean adulthood. However, adulthood is only really achieved through the gradual process of grow-ing, learning, and maturing. If you have not yet found solutions to your own conflicts and are not certain of your identity, the act of getting married will not provide them for you. You might end up feeling even more dependent and lost as all your time and energy are spent on household chores and raising a baby.

> *I have to do all the cooking. Sean says that's my job because he works all day. OK. Then I have to do all the mending and sewing because we can't afford to buy new clothes. I wanted to make some curtains for the baby's room, so I have to ask Sean for $10 to buy the fabric. He says I already spent the household allowance. I have to ask for an allowance just like I was a kid again. I had to beg for a lousy $10 to buy something nice for our baby.—Cindie, 18.*

Cindie's problem brings us to another major reason why couples split apart—*money.* A good number of young people enter mar-riage thinking that "love will conquer all" or that "money is not important." The reality is that no matter how good a job might seem, the money brought in may not be enough once the baby comes. Having a baby in a hospital can be extremely costly. Then the baby will need a crib, blankets, clothes, a bassinette, special food, special medical care, and playthings. In addition, there are the everyday expenses to consider, such as rent, furniture, car, clothes, medical bills, and food. Everything adds up, and often the weekly paycheck cannot be stretched to pay for all the necessities, much less for luxuries like a color TV or an occasional movie or dinner out. It's no wonder that many young people fight over how the money is spent.

> *I get furious with my husband every time he goes out with his friends. They play cards and he usually loses. How can he keep doing that when I don't have enough money to pay the electric bill or feed the baby?—Charlene, 19.*

Sometimes, the problem with money lies with how it is to be divided and shared. Many men expect that since they earn the money, it's theirs to spend as they please. Often a young man resents that his hard-earned salary disappears to pay bills, feed a baby, and support a wife.

Conversely, a teenage girl may expect that her husband will pay for everything willingly and that there should be enough money to make ends meet. Again, the expectations do not live up to the reality of what a marriage and a family demands both emotionally and financially.

Yet another misexpectation is the *amount of attention and time* you hope to receive from each other. Sometimes, there is too little time together—sometimes, too much.

> *My man says I'm crowding him. He wants*
> *more time out with the boys. It makes me feel*
> *like he doesn't want me and the baby no more.*
> *—Jollene, 15.*

Frequently, both husband and wife begin to feel trapped. A teenage father may find that his male friends are still very important to him. He may need their companionship to maintain his sense of separateness—that he has an identity outside of just being a husband and father.

A young father may feel, too, that his wife is giving all her attention and time to the new baby. He might feel unnecessary and unloved now that the baby is born. Some young men report feeling jealous of the child. The father may feel cast aside since he believes he no longer comes first in the relationship, and he might be irritated because the baby interferes with sexual activities.

Conversely, a young woman may have expected that her husband would spend all his free time with her. When he doesn't, she may feel rejected and unloved. When a young husband has the freedom to go out with friends while she must stay inside and tend to the baby, the young wife often feels trapped and abandoned.

When both partners are working, they may have the problem of not seeing enough of each other.

> *I'm a waitress and Joe works a swing shift at the warehouse. That means his schedule changes every few weeks. It's good because most of the time one of us is home to take care of the baby so we don't have to pay for daycare or a babysitter. But because we have different schedules, we hardly ever see each other and that's rough on us.—Darlene, 19.*

Still other marriages run into trouble because some people think that *faults will disappear* once the marriage license is signed. "He'll stop criticizing me." "He won't hit me once we're married." "He'll drop his other girlfriends." "He'll stop drinking once he has more responsibilities." If you see a fault in your partner's character, marriage will not change it. The stress that comes with marriage and parenthood may, in fact, make the problem worse. In general, the act of marriage will not solve any problem you have in your relationship with your boyfriend.

Some girls who become pregnant and want to marry, do so in hope of *binding their boyfriends closer* to them. They expect that marriage and the baby will solve their difficulties, and that their boyfriend's indifference will turn into devotion. This almost never works in the long run. A child can put a strain on even the most solid marital relationship. If the relationship is shaky to begin with, a baby may cause the marriage to break down.

The added responsibility of raising an infant can lead to frustration and anger which may result in either or both parents striking out at the child. If this happens, it may become necessary to place the child in a temporary foster home until the major problems are solved. Chapter 9 talks about this option.

Sometimes a marriage ends because two people *grow apart* as they mature and gain stronger self-images. Most people do not develop clear goals for themselves until their 20s. The expectations for themselves and their partners can change as a result.

Jesse was 18 when she became pregnant and married.

> *I married a man who was as different from my workaholic father as possible. I wanted some-*

*one who just wanted to stay at home and help
me raise a family. Now I see that Larry has no
ambition and I find that I want to travel and
meet exciting people, but I'm stuck in a small
town in a marriage I can't stand anymore.*

In general, if your differences are many—you have no common
background, have different religions or moral values, do not share
the same ideas about faithfulness, commitment, and parenting; or
if you disagree on how to handle money, divide chores, where to
live, spend leisure time, and make decisions—you need to spend
more time working out those differences before you commit to
marriage.

If the negative aspects of marriage outweigh the positive ones, it
may be better for you to explore the other options open to you,
such as adoption, foster care, raising the baby yourself, or abortion
if it is still early in your pregnancy.

What About Living Together?

Looking at the problems of marriage, many people wonder why
they should even bother getting married. You may look around
you and see many divorced parents. Marriage might seem empty—
nothing more than the piece of paper the marriage license is printed
on.

Furthermore, many people, maybe even some of your friends,
are living together. The relationship may seem to be working for
them. These days, living together is generally accepted. It might
even seem like a good idea, because if one of you decides to end the
relationship, all you have to do is leave. On the surface, it appears
to be a much easier alternative.

Problems are associated with living together, however, especially for the young woman and her child. If you are thinking about
moving in with your boyfriend, you may find that without the legal
tie of marriage, you have no right to anything your boyfriend
purchases while you are living together. For example, you may be

staying at home, cooking, and caring for the baby and your boyfriend while he goes out and works. In exchange, he pays for the rent, the furniture, the TV, the car, your clothes. If you decide to split up, legally he gets to keep everything. If you were married, you would be entitled to a fair share of everything accumulated during the marriage.

If he has a job that covers his health and/or life insurance, you and your baby can share no part of that if you are just living together. In other words, if you or your baby becomes ill, his insurance will not cover you. You are on your own.

Further, if your boyfriend is in an accident or becomes seriously ill and is unable to make decisions about his medical care, you will not be able to give consent for it. Nor will he be able to give consent for you in the same circumstances. You may not even be able to see each other while you are in the hospital unless you are legally married. Should your boyfriend suddenly die, leaving you and your child with no income, you would not receive his life insurance (unless he makes you beneficiary) nor any part of his accumulated social security.

Your baby's future could be jeopardized because, without marriage, your child is legally bereft. He or she may receive nothing from the father if you break up. He would not be required to provide child support unless he legally acknowledges paternity, or paternity is established through a blood test. This may involve your taking him to court. What is more, statistics show that court-ordered child support payments are usually very small, and most young fathers stop making even those small payments within two years.

When your child is old enough to ask questions, he or she may wonder why you didn't get married. Deep inside, your child may think that "Daddy didn't love Mommy enough to get married," or "They only stayed together because of me. They didn't love each other, so how could they love me?" In spite of society's growing acceptance of "illegitimate" children, a child can experience much self-doubt growing up with unanswered questions about his/her beginnings. Moreover, children often feel that they are the cause of their parents' problems, particularly if the parents break up.

A child needs a sense of permanency to grow up feeling secure. Besides, a child needs both parents in order to develop a distinct relationship with both sexes. Without this, a child may grow up feeling emotionally deprived and have difficulty making adjustments as he/she develops.

Sometimes, getting pregnant, getting married, and having a baby is too much for a young couple to cope with all at once. They may decide to postpone marriage until they are adjusted to living together and to the baby.

People often avoid marriage because, if there are difficulties, it's easier to escape from them when there are no legal ties. In thinking about your relationship to each other, you should consider why you feel this "escape hatch" is necessary. Do you believe that your relationship is only temporary? Are you unable to deal with stress or solve problems? What do you think is preventing you from committing to a permanent relationship, especially now that you will be sharing a child together?

In marriage, if there are problems, you and your partner are more likely to try to work them out because you expect to stay married. In working them out, you may find a renewed closeness that will help you understand and appreciate each other more. By overcoming a hurdle together, you gain more confidence in yourselves and each other. This strengthens your relationship and increases your commitment to your marriage.

The Three of You

Marrying while you are pregnant is a special situation. The major events of life are speeded up and compressed. You find out you are pregnant, decide to marry, and give birth to a baby all within a few months time.

The stresses you are under are immense. Your parents may or may not be able to help you out emotionally or financially. Whatever your personal situation is, it still comes down to the two of you and, after the baby is born, the three of you.

What makes a teenage marriage work? First, there has to be a degree of maturity and commitment to each other. Then you and your partner will have to deal with the changes in your lives as realistically as possible. This may mean scaling-down your expectations. You will probably have to work very hard and make sacrifices in the present in order to build a satisfying family life in the future.

It is also a good idea to do a lot of talking in the few months you have together before the baby comes. Adjusting to the realities of caring for a newborn will be easier if you and your husband have established some guidelines you both can agree upon. Talk over the questions listed earlier in this chapter, if you have not already had the chance to do so. It might be a good idea to review them again, since your expectations and realities can change once you are legally married.

It is usually the girl who brings up these subjects, for the woman is closer to the event of child-bearing and rearing. She thinks about it in much more concrete terms than he. Knowing what you can expect from one another will ease some of the stresses that come once the baby is born.

When you bring the baby home, you will find that your time is very much taken up by the continual care that a newborn infant needs. You are going to have to sharpen your organizational skills in order to get everything done and still have some time for yourself and for your husband.

Having the support of your parents can also help your marriage to work. Even though they may be against everything that has happened, they often come through during the rough times. After all, your mom and dad are a part of your extended family—they are the grandparents to your baby.

Most experts agree that the most important element in any marriage is *communication*. Talk to each other. Encourage each other to express both positive and negative feelings. Even more important, *listen* to each other. Try to put yourself in the other's place. Be sensitive to the other's feelings. Try to remain open to each other, even as you change and grow in the years to come.

It helps to see your situation as a joint effort. You are teammates trying to win at making a successful marriage. If you can accept your situation, continue to talk to each other about problems that arise daily, and reinforce each other as you strive toward mutual goals, you have a good chance of building a solid and lasting marriage.

EIGHT

ADOPTION

I never even considered adoption until my ninth month when a doctor suggested it to me. I wanted the best for my baby and adoption seemed like the answer.—Diana, 17.

I miss the baby and wonder how she's doing. Sometimes I feel terribly sad even though I know I did the right thing. I was just too young to be a good mother.—Eddi, 15.

It's too bad more people don't know about adoption. I didn't until my baby was two months old. By then I could see I wasn't making it as a parent and I was glad adoption was still open to me and the baby.—Sandy, 19.

"Is Adoption for Me?"

For the many girls who continue their pregnancies, but don't feel ready to take on the responsibilities of parenthood, adoption may be a good choice to make. Over 20,000 teenagers decide for adoption each year. Even though most unmarried girls keep their babies at home, 8 percent surrender their babies to adoptive parents who are not relatives.

Young mothers who choose adoption for their babies do so because they feel too young for motherhood, they don't have financial means, or they feel it is best for the child under the circumstances.

At first, I wanted to keep my baby and raise it. But as the time got closer, I realized that I just couldn't do it. It would mean a total change in my life and I wasn't prepared for it. So I decided to give my child up for adoption.—Miriam, 14.

It is not an easy decision to make. It means giving your rights as a parent over to another couple or family. Adoption is, therefore, a decision that requires serious thought. Most young women make this choice after long and careful consideration and much soul-searching.

In the recent past, before 1970, most girls surrendered their babies for adoption rather than keeping them and raising them at home. Of course, safe, legal abortion was not available to teenagers then. People's attitudes have changed about unwed mothers, too, and keeping the baby has become more acceptable.

As a result, many girls today don't consider adoption because they think that continuing their pregnancy means keeping the child.

There are several other reasons why adoption is not considered. One is the fear of being thought of as "selfish" or "cruel" if the baby is given to adoption. You may have friends or relatives who have asked, "How can you give up your own baby?" Perhaps you have asked yourself the same question.

If you foresee that you will have a difficult time financially and/or emotionally in raising a child to adulthood, or if you have plans for school or a career, giving up your baby for adoption may be the least "selfish" thing you can do. It can be an act of love.

It may be helpful to know that adoptive parents are very carefully selected by agencies. Adoptive parents are people who want to give your baby love, a good home, and a happy family life.

Some girls are concerned about their parents' reaction. A teenager may fear that her parents have the right to give the baby away or that they will try to claim the baby once the decision for adoption has been made. Only you (and the biological father of the baby) can give your baby up for adoption and, legally, your parents can't begin or stop adoption proceedings.

Another reason some girls don't ask about adoption is because they have heard that adoption agencies are "baby-snatchers" or that they will force you into a decision before you are ready. You can be reassured that this will not happen. The law states that you can't give up your baby for adoption until after it is born. (In some states, you cannot sign final adoption papers until three to ten days after the baby is born.) Adoption agencies provide counseling to help you in your decision. Their first concern is for you and your child. It is in their interest to help you make a decision you can live with.

If you are thinking about adoption, call or visit an adoption agency. Counselors there will be glad to talk with you, help you explore your feelings and answer any questions you might have. You might also want to talk with a clergyman or a rabbi. He or she may be able to help you sort out your feelings and answer some questions. Almost every religious organization can put you in touch with an adoption agency. Or you can find one listed in the Yellow Pages. Look under "Adoption Agencies" and "Social Service Organizations." You can also try calling your state, county, or local Department of Adoption or Child Welfare Agency.

Unlike marriage, which can change or end in divorce, adoption is final. This brings us to one last reason, and perhaps the major reason, why some young women don't consider adoption—the fear that they can never accept and live with the decision and will instead be haunted by feelings of guilt and regret.

Sometimes the conflict a young woman feels is complicated by the hope that circumstances in her life will change, making it possible to keep her child. She may delay her decision in the belief that she can maintain a relationship with her boyfriend through the baby—that once the child is born, he will want to be involved in raising it.

The reverse may also be true. For the teenager who feels emotionally and financially unprepared to raise a child, but whose boyfriend hopes to continue the relationship with her through this mutual bond, the pressure to consider keeping the baby may leave her undecided.

For the girl who has abandoned all hope of involvement with her boyfriend, there may be the expectation that her mother (or parents) will let her keep the baby once it is born and will offer some support after all.

When support from neither her boyfriend nor mother are forth-coming, and the young woman is alone with her dilemma, the reasons for giving up her baby may become painfully evident. There are likely to be feelings of anger and resentment toward the people she feels have abandoned her, guilt for bringing a child into the world whom she cannot care for, and feelings of emptiness and loss at giving up what she feels is a part of herself.

With the help of sensitive counseling, these feelings can be expressed and dealt with, and finally accepted, making it possible to find gratification in knowing her baby will have a good home with parents who can provide what is needed.

Dorothy, who was 16 when she gave up her baby for adoption, would probably agree.

I don't believe in abortion, so I had the baby. But I was only a sophomore in high school and too young to provide my baby with all the things he would need and want. I could never give him the things my parents gave me. So as hard as it was, adoption was the best thing for me to do for my baby. I know he's growing up now in a nice house and has two nice people as parents. When I remember that, I feel very good about my decision for adoption.

Adoption Agencies

Government-authorized adoption agencies are public or private organizations that can help you with all aspects of adoption. They provide counseling, handle all legal matters, assist you in finding a maternity home, help you get prenatal care, arrange for your delivery, and select the home where your baby will be placed. All matters are confidential and your name and the adoptive parents' names are kept secret.

The adoptive parents pay all fees for counseling, legal aid, and services to your child. The adoption agency can't give you financial assistance, but they can refer you to a social agency that might be able to help you.

You and your baby are of primary importance to an adoption agency. There are some advantages to independent adoptions, which will be discussed later in this chapter; but you should know that a doctor or lawyer who arranges the independent adoption considers the adoptive parents as his or her primary clients.

Some teenagers worry that an agency will place the baby in an orphanage or with undesirable people. The truth is, there are so many couples waiting today to become adoptive parents that your baby can be placed immediately in his or her new home. One study shows that there are twenty families waiting for each child who is put up for adoption. The average couple waits between two and five years to adopt a child, and they are very carefully selected.

An agency wants to make sure your baby is placed in a good home, one that is secure and loving, and the best match for your baby. Most likely, the adoptive parents are in their early 20s to mid-30s. The couple must show that they have been married long enough and that their marriage is happy and stable. Adoptive parents must be able to provide financial security for the baby, and they must have a large enough house or apartment so that the baby can have his or her own room (or if the couple already has children, the baby must be able to share a room with a child of the same sex). The home must also meet standards of neatness and organization. The adoptive parents also are required to take medical tests to prove they are healthy, and they must provide character references. Moreover, an agency caseworker will talk to the prospective parents to determine if there are any personal problems (alcoholism, marital conflicts, etc.) and whether they have the qualities of maturity and compassion to be loving parents to an adopted child.

Only after they have "passed" these requirements will a couple be considered as suitable adoptive parents.

You, too, have some say as to who the adoptive parents will be. You may choose in what religion you want your baby raised (in some states, the mother's faith must match the adoptive parents') and you can be matched for race or nationality. Agencies try to match babies and adoptive parents as closely as possible.

In many agencies, you can also request certain aspects of family life that you would like for your child. Do you want him or her raised in an active, outdoors family? A musical, artistic family? A quiet, intellectual family? There are no guarantees, but most agencies will try to place your baby in a home that comes as close as possible to your wishes.

Sometimes, a caseworker will describe the family to you, or will even describe several families and let you pick the one that seems best.

One reason a girl may not want to go to an agency is because she feels uneasy about the idea of "giving up the baby to strangers." In some instances, a social worker can arrange a meeting between you and the adoptive parents. Ask your agency if this is possible. If not, perhaps you can look for another agency.

In many cases, though, you can have some contact with the adoptive parents and even with your child. You can write a letter to them and/or your baby. Your social worker will see that the adoptive parents receive it. They can write to you through the agency and the letter will be given to you.

Once the baby is born, some girls write a letter to the baby and send along a gift. Your social worker will deliver both to your baby. This can help you feel connected to your child and his or her new family. Writing a letter to your baby can also let you explain why you decided for adoption and to say how you feel about him or her. Someday this letter may be very meaningful to your child.

Your name and address is kept secret from the adoptive family, just as theirs is kept secret from you. Laws regarding this may change, however. Thus, you might want to think about the possibility of meeting your child in the future. Some agencies may ask for that information now in preparation for any change in the law.

When your baby is born, you will fill in a birth certificate with your name and the biological father's name. This is then sealed and filed away. It cannot be seen except by a court order. Then a new certificate is issued with the adoptive parents' names.

As mentioned before, you won't sign a final adoption form until after your baby is born and you have had a chance to rest and recuperate. However, if you still need a few days or a few weeks to think about it, you can sign a "release form" which allows the agency to take the baby out of the hospital and into a foster home. This does not mean that you have signed away your rights as a parent. You can still change your mind.

When you have definitely decided for adoption, you will be given "relinquishment papers" to sign. Once you have signed these papers, the adoption is considered final and binding. You no longer have any legal rights to, or responsibilities for, your child.

The father of your baby has certain legal rights, too. Later on in this chapter, in the section called, "What About My Boyfriend," we discuss his involvement in the adoption procedure.

Since the details of the law are different in every state, it is best to find out in advance what is required. Be sure to read everything very carefully before you sign. If there is something you don't understand, ask your counselor or social worker about it. Keep copies of everything you sign.

Even though the intent of the law is to give you plenty of time to make a decision about adoption, arriving at a decision as early as possible gives you the opportunity to shop around for the best agency before the baby is born. It gives the agency enough time to select the best home available and insures the baby a smooth transition into his or her adoptive home.

Independent Adoptions

An independent adoption is one that is made through an "independent" person, such as a doctor or lawyer, rather than through an agency. In this case, the doctor or lawyer may know of a couple who wish to adopt a baby. Some doctors and lawyers have a list of clients who are hoping to adopt. A teenager may learn of such a doctor or lawyer from her own physician, from her parents' lawyer, or from a counselor.

Some teenagers feel that the main advantage in an independent adoption arrangement is that they have a greater chance of knowing or meeting the people who will adopt the baby. It is possible that you or your parents may have friends or relatives who might want to adopt the baby. This can be achieved with the help of a lawyer who can make the legal arrangements for an independent adoption. Adoption by relatives is common and is considered a form of independent adoption; however, there are some special considerations that are dealt with in the following section.

Independent adoption is not allowed in some states, although it is in most. To be legal in the states that allow independent adoptions, the adoption must be presented before and approved by a judge in your state's family or surrogate court.

It is advisable to have a reputable lawyer to represent you. Since the lawyer representing the adoptive parents will put their interests first, it is helpful to have your own lawyer. Your lawyer can explain the legal procedures and your rights, such as your state's legal waiting period. Your lawyer can also protect you against possible fraud, forged documents, or signing the release form under duress (that is, being pressured to relinquish against your free will). Whereas an adoption agency will handle all legal matters concerning an adoption, if you decide for an independent adoption you are on your own. Some states require a "law guardian" for girls under the age of 18. To find a lawyer, contact your state's Bar Association, the Department of Probation, Family Court, or Legal Aid. A social caseworker can also help you find a lawyer.

As you know, an adoption agency carefully selects the adoptive parents *before* the baby can be placed in their home. In an independent adoption, the family is not studied until *after* the baby has been placed. This can cause problems for you, and especially for your baby, if the family is found unfit by the state.

At the time an independent adoption is arranged, adoptive parents will agree to pay for your legal, medical, and hospital bills. Sometimes, they even pay for your living expenses until the baby is born. This is legal; however, any money or gifts given to you must be reported to the court.

On occasion, a pregnant girl will be offered large sums of money or expensive gifts to give up her baby. If these payments are not reported or approved by your state's court, the "adoption" can be considered illegal.

Receiving money while still pregnant may seem attractive, but even in a legal arrangement, a teenager may feel "obligated" to give her baby up to the people who have been paying her expenses. After the baby is born, a young woman might want to change her mind, but may be pressured not to. You *do* have the right to change your mind, and legally you do not have to repay these expenses.

If you decide to go ahead with an independent adoption, after your baby has been born, you will sign a "take into care" form. This is not a final paper, but will allow the prospective adoptive parents to take the baby home while the state study takes place. This study usually takes six to eight weeks. Up to that time, you or the adoptive parents can have a change of mind.

After the study is completed and the family is approved by the court, you will sign a "consent for adoption" form, naming the two people who will become the baby's new parents. This paper must be signed in the presence of a representative of your state's Department of Social Services. Once the adoption is final, you can no longer ask for your child back.

For some teenagers, it may be important to know the adoptive parents by name, and perhaps even know where they live, particularly if it is in the same town or neighborhood. Other teenagers prefer not to know, because they find it too painful to be in such close contact with the child and the adoptive parents. Only you can decide how you would feel.

One major disadvantage to independent adoptions is the lack of decision-making counseling.

> *I felt terribly guilty about giving up my baby and accepting money to pay for my medical bills. It made me feel like I was selling my baby or something. But my parents aren't rich and were glad to have the help. There was no way I could have taken care of it myself. I met the family who adopted my baby, but then they*

> *moved away. I don't know where they are, and I'll probably never see my baby again. I thought about her all the time and even had nightmares. Finally, I went to a counselor, and she helped me quite a bit. I can accept what happened a little better now.—Melissa, 16.*

Because of the potential for mixed feelings about the many aspects of independent adoption, finding a professional counselor can help you anticipate and sort out your feelings before making a decision and can reduce the impact of the negative feelings that you may experience afterwards.

In one study, it was found that the majority of young women who felt they made the right decision for adoption had received counseling. They felt they had made their own decision and were not pressured into it.

There are advantages and disadvantages to both arrangements. It's up to you, considering your special circumstances, to decide which will be best for you and your baby.

Adoption by Relatives

Some teenagers decide to have their babies adopted by a relative. In fact, of the 13 percent of babies born to unmarried teenage mothers who are adopted, 5 percent are ultimately adopted by a member of the family.

Adoption by a relative often occurs a year or two after the baby is born. Sometimes it happens with young married couples who find they cannot cope with raising a baby, or who divorce.

Adoption by a relative is considered to be a form of independent adoption. The same guidelines and laws apply as were discussed in the previous section, "Independent Adoptions."

Even though you may give your baby up for adoption to a close relative, the adoption is still final. Legally, you have no more rights to your child than you would by having your baby adopted by strangers.

If you are thinking about letting relatives adopt your baby, be sure to talk it over with them. All of you must understand that the adoption will have to be presented in court. You should each get a lawyer, who can explain your state's legal procedures as well as your respective rights and obligations. Your relatives will have to submit to an agency study before the adoption can be finalized.

There are many positive aspects to adoption by relatives. You know the people who will adopt your baby. You might even know them well and enjoy a close relationship.

It can also be reassuring to know where your child is and the circumstances in which he or she is growing up.

Adoption by relatives can also cause pain or envy, for it may hurt to see your child growing up with other people, even people you know and love.

Brooke was 17 when she surrendered her child for adoption.

> *My older cousin and her husband adopted my baby girl, since they couldn't have children themselves. I remember visiting them and watching my baby's whole face light up when my cousin picked her up. She never did that for me. Of course, she didn't know I was her birth mother and that's the way it should be, but still, I remember feeling the pain inside.*

Further, there is the potential for lifelong conflict between you and your relatives, which could be painful and confusing for your child.

There may be disagreements among you on what the child should be told about his or her beginnings. You may both agree on what to tell the child, but later you may change your mind. There may be disagreements, too, on many other issues of parenting, which can leave a child feeling confused and divided.

Almost every mother wants her baby to have the best, and adoption by a relative may be the best choice to make in your circumstance. Before deciding on *any* adoption arrangement, it's a good idea to talk with an adoption counselor. Call an adoption agency and ask to speak with one. A trained adoption counselor can help you make the best decision for you and your baby, as well as assist you in carrying out your decision.

"What About My Boyfriend?"

In 1972, the Supreme Court ruled that an unwed father has legal rights to his child. Basically, the law states that any unwed father, even a teenage father, has the right to a hearing before his biological child can be taken away or surrendered in adoption.

This means that the father of your child must at least be notified if you wish to go ahead with an adoption. Without this, the biological father of your baby may return at some future time and disrupt a successful adoption by demanding his child back. This can be extremely painful to you, the adoptive parents, and especially your child.

It is very important that he is informed and that he signs the necessary papers.

Once the biological father knows of the adoption plans, he can either disagree with the plans, deny that he is the father, waive (give up) his rights in writing, or agree with the plans and sign the relinquishment for adoption. Most often, the father agrees with the plans.

Sometimes a girl will not know who the father is or won't know where he is. It's very important for your baby's future to be honest with your caseworker and give all the information you can. The adoption agency must show that they have done everything possible to locate the biological father before the adoption can take place. If he cannot be found, or if he does not respond when notified, the court can provide a ruling which allows the adoption to take place without the biological father's written consent.

Once his parental rights have been waived by the court, or he agrees to the adoption in writing, the father no longer has any rights to or responsibilities for his child.

Some girls are worried that a boyfriend will try to stop an adoption or will try to take the baby himself. If you cannot come to a private agreement with the father of your baby, the case will be decided by a judge. Before the court will decide in his favor, and since your child's welfare is the state's first concern, the young man will have to show that he can properly support a child and provide a good, stable home. A teenage boy can rarely meet these qualifications.

Other girls may not want the boyfriend to know about the pregnancy and/or the adoption because they feel angry or hurt. If this is the case with you, you do not have to talk to your boyfriend yourself. Let your adoption caseworker know who he is, and she can then let him know of your wishes in the matter and discuss the situation with him, thereby giving your child the best chance for a smooth adoption.

In the majority of cases, the young man agrees to the adoption. Most teenage fathers also feel they are too young to be parents and want the best opportunity possible for the child, just as you do.

If you are on good terms with your boyfriend, discussing the adoption option with him will probably make him feel more involved and help him to better understand and accept the decision.

Accepting the Adoption Decision

Getting pregnant is an enormous event in any woman's life. Carrying a child within her until birth is a profound experience, filled with complex emotions and physical changes. Giving birth for the first time brings feelings, perhaps both positive and negative, that may change her view of life—no matter what the circumstances were surrounding her pregnancy or what decision she makes for herself and the child.

For many women, it makes giving up the baby for adoption a difficult decision to reach. It takes a strong conviction that it is the right decision for the child. It often means putting the baby's needs before their own.

"If this is the right decision," many teenagers ask, "why does it hurt so much?"

In the past, a major reason for the pain of surrendering a baby for adoption was that the young mother was not allowed to see her child before it was taken away.

Most social workers today believe it is good to let a young mother see, hold, and even breast-feed her baby before adoption.

> *I stayed in the hospital for three days and breast-fed my baby before he was adopted. I was so glad that he got to know me and I got to know him. It was wonderful knowing he was alive and healthy. That really helped me when the time came for his new parents to pick him up.—Morgan, 16.*

Seeing your baby and holding him or her even for a little while can act as a "sealer," a reconfirmation that you made the right decision.

> *When I was allowed to hold the baby, I felt so clumsy and the baby seemed so fragile, like it would break or something. I knew then that I definitely wasn't ready to be a mother and I was glad the baby was going to someone who really wanted him.—Charleene, 17.*

Some girls may feel that seeing the baby would make them change their minds. It might. But it may also calm any doubts or questions you had about the baby you gave birth to before surrendering it, thereby bringing a sense of closure to your experience.

No one should force you to see the child if you do not want to. It's your decision to make as you think best. It's good to know, though, that you do have a choice in this very important matter.

In the days and weeks following the adoption, there will be many adjustments to be made. There may be relief that the experience is behind you or there may be a mourning period in which there is a real sense of emptiness inside. Probably there will be both. Brief periods of depression sometimes occur as the anniversary of the baby's birth approaches.

Many women who have been through the experience report that

the sense of emptiness and loss are eased when they eventually are old enough to have a child they can plan for and raise.

If possible, talk to other women who have given up a baby for adoption. Hearing how they adjusted to their experience may help you feel less alone. Your agency caseworker may be able to put you in touch with other teenagers.

Keep in touch with your adoption counselor. Don't be embarrassed to call after the adoption is final. A counselor can help you through the adjustment period by providing emotional support.

We mentioned that many teenage mothers write a letter to their baby or to the adoptive parents to express their deepest feelings. You needn't send the letter. Sometimes just putting your thoughts and feelings down on paper can help.

Surrendering a baby for adoption shows a sense of caring and responsibility toward the child. It is not an easy decision to make. Yet adoption can provide you and your baby each the opportunity to start life anew.

NINE

FOSTER CARE

Foster care is working out well for me. I was 16 when I had Julie. I didn't have any money and knew I had to finish high school to get a job. But I didn't want to give up my baby! Now a foster family takes care of Julie and I visit her three or four times a week. When I'm 18, and have a job, I plan to take Julie back and raise her myself.—Maria, 17.

I've missed out on so much of Brian's development. His foster parents were with him when he took his first steps. When I finally will be able to keep him, he'll seem like someone else's child.—Suzy, 15.

Dealing with a baby full-time was getting too much for me. I know I did things that weren't good for the baby. I had to get some help. So the baby is in foster care.—Sharon, 18.

What Is Foster Care?

Foster care is a way for people to receive temporary help when they can't take care of their children just yet, but believe they will be able to in the near future. A foster family cares for the child on a short-term basis until the birth mother (or birth parents) are ready to take the child back.

Unlike adoption, you are legally the child's mother and you will most likely meet the couple who will take care of your child. In fact, you will probably be required to visit the foster family and your baby regularly.

Foster care is sometimes used by a single teenager who hasn't yet decided between adoption and raising the child herself. By putting the baby in a foster home for a few weeks, she has more time to make this very important decision.

Occasionally, if the biological father won't sign the adoption papers, foster care is used for a short time until a court ruling can decide where the baby can be best placed on a permanent basis.

Foster care is also used by parents with children of all ages who find that they cannot cope with the many problems and responsibilities that are part of child-rearing. For some, the frustration builds to a point where they neglect or abuse their child. To protect the child, the state often must place him or her in a foster home.

In many cases, though, when a teenager voluntarily gives up her child to a foster home, it is because she wants to keep her baby, but needs time to complete high school, get married, find a job, and/or have a place to live before she can begin to take on the full responsibility of raising the baby herself.

Foster homes are carefully selected by public and private social service agencies. People who become foster parents are chosen because they have stable, happy marriages, have a secure job and income, enjoy children, and know how to take care of them. Foster parents very often have children of their own.

As with potential adoptive parents, foster parents must go through a detailed investigation by the social agency. Is their home clean, organized, and well run? Are the parents emotionally balanced? Are there any family problems?

Foster parents usually are studied as carefully as adoptive parents. In addition, foster parents are asked how they will act toward a child who will be with them only temporarily. Can they give the baby affection and emotional security, yet still be able to give him or her up when it is time? Will they welcome visits by the birth mother?

In many ways, being a foster parent is more difficult than being an adoptive parent. It takes a very special person to love and care for a child knowing that he or she will ultimately return to the birth mother, or be adopted by other people. Because this emotional involvement is difficult to balance, most foster parents request time limits on how long they feel they can keep a child. Three to six months is common for babies.

Foster parents have many responsibilities in taking care of your baby. Because you have rights to your child, you have responsibilities, too. You (and possibly the baby's father) will be required to visit your child regularly, and you may be asked to help out financially. Foster care parents are given a small amount of money by the state to help pay for your baby's food, clothing, shelter, and playthings. Since this money is rarely enough, many foster parents contribute to the baby's care themselves, or they rely on help from the birth parents. Since you are considered the baby's parent, you must show that you want to be an active participant in your baby's life.

Unfortunately, young mothers often leave their babies in foster care too long. Frequently, the child is moved from home to home while the birth mother struggles with her own problems. This can interfere with normal emotional development in a child. Children need someone to depend on during infancy in order to feel secure. If you feel you are not yet ready to become a full-time parent and are unable to make plans to provide for your child in the near future, you may decide that the best alternative for your baby is adoption.

Foster care works best for a baby if it lasts only for a limited time, and when the birth mother shows her love for her baby by visiting often, and by organizing her life so that she can take over the child's care as soon as possible.

Foster Care Placement

You can place your child in a foster home by contacting a social agency. Any number of organizations can help you. Look in your telephone directory under "United Community Services" and your state's "Department of Child Welfare." Most religious organizations can help you, too, as can many adoption agencies and maternity homes. A doctor or a lawyer may also be able to refer you to a foster care agency.

It is better to start looking for an agency before your baby is born. You are not obligated by telephoning or visiting a foster care or an adoption agency. By getting as much information as you can in advance, you will have more time to make an unhurried, thoughtful decision.

A foster care counselor or social worker will be glad to talk with you and answer your questions. If you do decide for foster care, they can help you understand how to fill in the various forms and assist you in making present and future arrangements for yourself and your baby.

The agency makes the final decision where your baby will be placed, but you can request that your child be placed in a home that shares your religious faith, or in a family of your own race and nationality. Since many more girls use foster care than choose adoption, and since there are fewer foster parents available than adoptive parents, your choice of foster homes may be limited. Because of this, an agency cannot guarantee that all your requests will be fulfilled, but they will do their best to place your child in a home that will make you and your baby happy.

Jane, who is 19, had a very positive experience with the foster family who took care of her baby.

> *Tommy's foster mom is a great person. She took very good care of him and taught me a lot, too! She showed me how to feed him and change diapers and all sorts of things about babies I never knew before. Even though Tommy is living with me now, I still go back to visit her and her children. They're kind of my second family and I really love them.*

Your Legal Rights Under Foster Care

When you decide for foster care, you are *temporarily* giving your baby to a family who will care for and raise your child. But you are legally the baby's mother. The child keeps the full name you have chosen for him or her.

At the time that you decide for foster care, you (and the baby's father) must sign a foster care agreement form. This gives an authorized agency the right to become the legal guardian of your child.

The foster care agreement form will include such items as how often you should visit your child, how long your child will be kept with a foster family, how much money you may have to contribute to the foster care, and how many times you must see your agency caseworker.

This form is not an adoption or a relinquishment agreement. Your parents cannot sign a foster agreement form since, legally, they have no rights to your baby. The father of the baby, however, does have rights to his child. He must sign the foster care papers. If the father or his whereabouts is unknown, or if he refuses to admit his paternity, consent for foster care may have to be decided by the court. For more detailed information, read "What About My Boyfriend?" in the chapter on adoption.

It is very important that you understand everything you sign. If you are confused or don't completely understand any part of the agreement, ask your social worker or a lawyer to explain it to you. To find a lawyer you can afford, look in the Yellow Pages under "Lawyers" or "Lawyer Referral Services."

Be sure to keep copies of everything you sign. These forms are very important, as are all legal papers you sign.

When the forms are completed, the custody of your child will be given to the social agency that will, in turn, place your baby with an acceptable family as soon as possible.

It is extremely important to understand that when you sign the foster care form, you are making a promise to *do* what you have agreed to do. If you have signed the form saying you will visit your baby every Saturday afternoon, then you must do so. If you do not take your written promise seriously, there is a chance you might lose your child permanently.

Angela, who was 17, lost her baby because she visited the child only once in a while, and eventually stopped visiting altogether. The court decided that the child would be better off if she were adopted by a family who could give her full attention and care.

Although the baby does indeed belong to you, some of your responsibilities and rights are transferred to the foster parents and the foster care agency.

For example, foster parents can raise and care for the baby as they think best even if you disagree with them. Further, it is up to the foster care agency to decide in which home your baby should be placed. They can move your child to another home without your permission. They can limit your access to the baby, or even end your rights as a parent if you have not fulfilled your part of the foster care agreement—or, if it can be shown through your actions that you are an unfit mother. In any event, before permanent action is taken you will be notified, and you do have the right to legal appeal.

Yes, your baby is still really yours; but with rights come responsibilities. If you are willing and able to be a dependable and caring mother to your baby while he or she is in foster care, then it's likely you will be a successful mother once your baby is home with you.

Informal Foster Care

Sometimes, a teenage mother may have a friend or a relative who would like to take care of the baby until the teenager is ready to care for the child herself. You can agree to let your baby live with your parents, an aunt and uncle, an older sister and her husband, your boyfriend's parents, or friends of your family. This is called informal or private foster care.

There is no need to go through a court procedure or to sign foster care papers. Only if the "informal foster parent" takes the baby after birth from the hospital, must you sign a release form. This form is not a foster care or an adoption agreement. Even if your own mother takes the baby from the hospital, you will be required to sign the release form. This is for your protection in order to keep your full rights as the baby's legal mother. If you take the baby home yourself, and later give him or her to the informal foster parents, no legal papers have to be signed.

Any kind of agreement you wish to make—how often you'd like to visit your child, when you think you'll be ready to take back your child, whether you will contribute money toward your child's care—is made between you and the people who will raise your child.

However, even in an informal foster care arrangement, your baby may be taken away by the state if it can be proven that you have abandoned or abused your child. It is important for you to show a strong interest in your child's welfare and to be an active mother. Even though your child may be living with friends or relatives, your child needs to know that you are the mother and that you love and care about him or her.

In some cases, the informal foster parents may be able to receive money from the government to help pay for your baby's necessities. It is possible that relatives may be eligible for this financial assistance, even if the baby's foster parents are your own parents and you are living at home with them. To learn more, contact your state's Department of Child Welfare or any social service agency.

Although the family you choose to raise your baby temporarily is not first screened by an agency, one major advantage of informal foster care is already knowing the people who will be caring for your child. In many cases, the young mother has a good relationship with the friend or relative and knows that her baby will be well cared for.

There may be some disagreements as to how your child is being raised. This can occur even when strangers become the foster parents. It will be important to work your feelings out. A foster care counselor or your caseworker can help.

There are other alternative foster care arrangements that might be available to you. These include being placed in a foster home *yourself* along with your child, or family day care where you place your baby with a foster family during the day while you work or go to school. These choices are not offered everywhere, or at all times, but it is a good idea to ask your caseworker about them.

Many times informal foster care works well for everyone concerned, especially when the people involved care about each other, and do their best to make a smooth transition from foster care to care by the birth mother herself.

"Is Foster Care for Me?"

Each teenage mother is a special person with a unique set of circumstances. Foster care works well for many young mothers and their babies; for others, foster care is used as a last resort, when all else fails.

Half the time, foster homes are used only after a child has been neglected or abused by its birth parent. This happens whether a teenager is married or is raising the child herself. Under even the best circumstances, parenting is difficult. The demands of caring for a young child can bring on exhaustion, frustration, and resentment. Angry feelings can get out of control and can lead to physical or psychological abuse of the child.

School-age mothers have greater problems because they most often have no husband, little money, and stressful life circumstances. A teenage mother may feel alone and desperate—unable to cope with her situation.

If you feel that you cannot control your angry impulses toward your baby, if you think you may hurt your child, or if you have already, get in touch with a social agency, or with "Parents Anonymous." Look in the Yellow Pages under "Parental Stress" or "Child Abuse." There may be a hot line in your area. They will put you in touch with someone who will help you and your baby. They are not set up to judge you, but to help you understand your behavior and help you change it. Counseling and the support of other women who have had the same problem can be important in helping you to learn how to be a better parent to your baby.

Babies can be hurt psychologically if they are shuttled from foster home to foster home. This often happens when the young mother can't—or won't—make up her mind about adoption.

Jill is an example. Pregnant at 16, she first wanted to give the baby up for adoption. But after the baby was born, she wanted to keep him. She did for six weeks, but when the constant care became too much for her she gave the baby to a foster home. Two months later, she wanted him back. She kept him for a few months but often neglected him. The state said it would be better if the baby were adopted, but Jill refused to sign the relinquishment papers. The child was placed with another foster family who agreed to keep him for twelve months. When the year was up, the baby had to be placed in a third foster home. Jill would not yet surrender the baby for adoption, although she rarely visited him. The child now is five years old and has been in seven foster homes. He has bad nightmares and feels that no one loves him.

A baby needs security and a sense of permanence. Every child needs to know that he or she belongs to someone.

If you feel troubled, or unable to give the *continuous* love and care your baby needs, foster care may not be for you. Your baby's future may be more secure in an adoptive home.

Long-term foster care when the birth mother is absent, neglectful, or abusive, leaves the child in a kind of limbo, often resulting in psychological or physical damage.

There are many evident advantages to foster care—the mother legally keeps her baby, she can finish school or find a job while her baby is being cared for, and she can take time to grow and set some goals for her baby and herself. For the child, short-term foster care can be helpful, because he is raised by people who are experienced in parenting, while his own mother remains an important part of his life.

Foster care can be right for you if you are committed to preparing now for that day in the near future when you take custody of your baby and become his or her full-time mother.

TEN

KEEPING THE BABY

I knew from the beginning that I would keep my baby. I really wanted to be a mother. I think that's the most important thing in the world. It's hard work, but there's nothing I'd rather do than be with my little Jennie.—Lynn, 16.

It was really hard going to school while I was pregnant. I felt so different, like everyone was staring at me. But once I saw my little girl in the delivery room and held her in my arms, I knew I had made the right decision.—Patti, 15.

I thought I'd love having a baby. But sometimes, I can't stand to be with him. I'd rather be out having fun with friends.—Meryl, 17.

Am I Making the Right Decision?

Continuing your pregnancy and keeping your baby is at once the simplest and most complex decision to make.

It is simple because it seems you don't have to do anything. You don't have to make an appointment for an abortion. You don't have to make plans to get married. You don't have to contact an agency for adoption or foster care. You don't even have to get a pregnancy test. You can just let things happen.

It's complex because no matter how much any young woman prepares for motherhood, she can never anticipate all of the changes having a baby will bring in her life. Some women describe the change as an inner shift in their image of themselves. They move from "childhood"—that is, being someone who still looks to parents to take care of them—to "parenthood," where they must now provide for another human being.

When a teenager is still dependent upon her own parents, having an infant who is dependent upon her can result in some blurring of her image of herself in the role of "mother." Young women who make the decision to keep the baby usually need a lot of help from their own families to successfully raise the child.

Statistically, more unwed teenagers choose abortion, but, in 1978, over 360,000 babies were born to teenagers who weren't married. And each year, this number is growing.

There are many reasons why a young woman chooses to keep her baby and raise it as a single parent.

One of the reasons most frequently reported by teenagers is their belief that they will have "something of their own" that no one can take from them. Perhaps you have thought to yourself, "I want a baby so that I will have someone to love who will love me back." Underneath this feeling is often the sense of being unloved. They feel that having a baby will insure that they will never feel unloved again.

The miraculous event of producing a new human being can fill a young mother with tender, loving feelings toward her newborn. Yet, some mothers say that they felt surprisingly unloving toward their babies until they had spent enough time caring for their child to develop a deep attachment.

Some of this feeling may come from the way newborns look. They are tiny, wrinkled, and sometimes shriveled. Often they are red, bruised, or swollen. They appear to be out of proportion—large heads and small bodies. Their eyes are unfocused and they have no control yet over their bodies.

> *I tell you, it's nothing like what you see on TV!—Della, 15.*

It takes several months before babies begin to fulfill adolescent expectations of chubby, cheerful, bright-eyed children.

What surprises many young mothers is the fact that infants are

不

dependent upon them to provide love, but babies can't return it. Children must experience love first before they can return it. This is a long process. It takes years before a child can begin to consider another person's needs and try to meet them.

So, there is sometimes deep disappointment that the fantasy of having someone to love who will return love doesn't come true. Instead, the young mother can feel overburdened by having to do all the giving and may feel even more unloved than before.

Since part of the fantasy is the expectation that she will be a better mother to her child than her own mother has been to her, a teenager may feel terrible if she is not a "perfect" mother all the time.

Yet motherhood is often difficult and demanding. Parenting is a full-time job. It's 24 hours a day, 7 days a week, 365 days a year. No weekends off. No summer vacations. Most mothers have times when they feel resentful toward their children. It doesn't mean they aren't good mothers. It just means they are human beings with limits to their endurance.

"But I love children," you might say, "I babysit all the time. I know how to dress them and feed them. I've done all that. It's not hard. I love dressing them up and playing with them."

This is in your favor and will help to balance out the more difficult aspects of childcare. Yet, mothers of every age have trouble keeping up with the endless chores. Almost every mother of an infant has trouble coping with physical exhaustion. Most young mothers say that their lives revolve around the demands of the baby.

As a result, almost three-fourths of unmarried teenage mothers turn to their own mothers for physical, emotional, and financial assistance. Many girls find that, with a baby, they need their parents more than ever. Suddenly, a teenager can feel very dependent again.

> *I couldn't wait to have my baby because I wanted my parents to see me as an adult. But I couldn't deal with doing everything for the*

> *baby myself. I was dead after coming home
> from school. I needed money. I dreaded spend-
> ing my evening with a screaming baby. My
> mom did most of it, and she let me know about
> it. She made me feel like I couldn't do anything.*
> —Corrine, 17.

For the teenager who expected to gain independence from her mother, the realization that she is even more dependent is a painful blow.

Sometimes a teenage girl will continue her pregnancy because someone important in her life wants her to do so. You might feel pressured by your parents, your boyfriend, or even your friends.

They each will have their own reasons for wanting you to keep the baby. For some families, abortion is not an option because of religious or personal beliefs. Occasionally, some mothers may really want a baby themselves and get their wish fulfilled through their daughter's having the baby. Some boyfriends want a baby so they can show the child off and brag about their "manhood." Some friends may like it because they can enjoy some of the benefits of motherhood without the responsibilities.

You will need to ask yourself if these are strong enough reasons for you to keep your baby and raise it yourself.

The teenagers who find the most satisfaction in their choice for motherhood are the ones who are very sure that having a baby will meet their primary goal in life—motherhood—with no other presently competing goals such as higher education, travel, or career.

Motherhood must be an achievement in itself and not a means of escaping from home, gaining love and acceptance, or winning a battle with a boyfriend or parents. If giving birth is seen as a way to change the minds of important people who oppose the decision, deep disappointment may follow.

Most importantly, a teenager must have a degree of maturity that makes her able to look realistically at her life situation and honestly conclude that she has the necessary emotional and financial support from family, boyfriend, relatives, friends, and/or social agencies.

The decision to keep and raise a child requires a commitment strong enough to carry you through the difficult times that all parents experience when the responsibilities of parenthood make them feel unappreciated, confused, and even cheated by their choice.

All parents occasionally long for the carefree days when they only had to think about their own needs and pleasures. During these times, it is the deep conviction that parenthood is what they wanted most, and freely chose after careful consideration, that makes the difference between feeling trapped and discouraged or basically optimistic about their lives and their future.

Preparing for Your Baby

Keeping your baby may be the right decision for you. If so, it will be important to plan ahead as much as you can before the baby is born.

In the next chapter, we'll discuss the plans you should make concerning your physical care during the nine months of pregnancy and childbirth. Now let's take a look at some of the practical considerations you should think about before and after the baby comes.

Do you know where you will live during your pregnancy and after your baby is born? Can you stay at home? If not, have you begun looking for an apartment, either to rent on your own or to share with a roommate? Is there a maternity home where you can stay? To find a maternity home, check the back of this book, or look in the Yellow Pages under "Homes—Institutional" and "Social Service Organizations." The Florence Crittenton Foundation and The Salvation Army can help you. Most religious organizations can also refer you to a maternity home.

How will you support yourself? Will you be able to take on a job or complete school after the baby is born? If so, do you have someone to look after your baby while you are working or in class? Is the father of the child prepared to make child support payments? How much? Can your parents assist you?

Your expenses will be increased once the baby is born. Have you priced a crib, a bassinet, a high chair, a carriage? Baby food and formula are expensive, too. Diapers are usually a major expense. They cost much more than people think. What about clothing for your child? Can you afford playthings? By reading a book on baby care, you can learn just what you will need to have on hand when the baby comes home.

Most young mothers have to work very hard to pay for the necessities. There is usually little left over for new clothes or a night out.

Many teenagers are willing to put the baby's needs before their own. Even so, there will be times when you may feel envious of friends who can afford nice things for themselves that are no longer possible for you to have. It is important to anticipate these feelings so that you are prepared to deal with them when the time comes.

Changing Relationships

During your pregnancy, you will experience many changes. As you watch for and feel the changes in your body, you may also feel changes emotionally. You may begin to feel vulnerable and dependent and want to be cared for by others. You may feel like crying without knowing why. These are normal feelings during pregnancy.

Pregnancy usually brings a lot of interest and attention from others. Parents will be concerned for your health. Your boyfriend may become more tender and considerate. Girlfriends want to know what it feels like to be pregnant.

After the baby is born, you may sense that everything has changed. *You* are no longer the center of attention, the *baby* is!

I couldn't believe it. While I was pregnant, my mother was so nice to me. She wouldn't let Dad yell at me because I might get upset. She made sure I got plenty of rest and ate right and all that stuff. Then after the baby was born, pow! It was like I wasn't there. Everyone paid attention to the kid and I didn't count anymore.—Gail, 16.

There may be other changes as well. If you remain at home and receive help from your parents, you may be grateful and at the same time resentful, because, although you, too, are now a mother, your mother may still treat you like a child, directing you how to care for your baby. Because she is experienced, it may be a relief to have her show you how to handle your baby and explain some of the baby's behavior that concerns or confuses you. At the same time, you may feel that she takes charge too much or does things differently from the way you do. This can lead to tensions and conflicts between you.

In some instances, parents may resent having to take the baby into their home. Your mother may be at the point in her life where she is looking forward to freedom from the responsibilities of children. Then, suddenly, she is faced with bringing up another baby. Your father, too, may resent a new financial responsibility.

Brothers and sisters may or may not be helpful. If they feel envious of, or displaced by the newcomer, they may take it out on the baby or on you.

> *My nine year old brother really hates me. He keeps telling the baby that I'm her big sister and that Mom is her real mother. I want to strangle him.—Catherine, 16.*

Yet, many mothers and daughters gain new respect for each other as they cooperate and share child care tasks. Their relationship grows stronger.

> *Having my baby really brought me close to my own mother. I understand her so much better now—everything she went through with my brother and me. She supports me with a lot of love and that's very good for my baby, too.— Susan, 18.*

If you move into your boyfriend's parents' home, there may be similar adjustments intensified by the fact that you must fit yourself and your baby into a family that is not your own. This may make you feel dependent upon their generosity and good will, and even more so on the good will of your boyfriend.

The teenage mother who moves out of her parents' home will have more control over how she raises her baby. She will also have more responsibility. She may periodically need some experienced adult to turn to for advice and relief from child care.

The relationship you have with your boyfriend may also change. When the focus of your time together changes from dating, school, parties, friends, and fun, to the more serious business of parenting, boys sometimes feel trapped in a role they are not ready for. When this happens, the strain may be too much and the relationship falls apart.

If the relationship has been long and stable, pregnancy sometimes brings a couple closer together. If there is a long-term commitment, even teenage couples can manage to raise a child together. Having help from one or both families makes it easier.

Girlfriends usually get excited about a baby. They may want to practice being mothers by doing things for your baby. But often, when the novelty wears off, you find that they cannot appreciate the importance of the many daily events that make having a baby so rewarding. You may find that your interests have changed and you really don't have that much in common anymore.

The biggest change will probably happen within you. Having a baby is a challenge. It tests your ability to learn new skills, to cope with stress, and to make complicated decisions on your own. As you gain mastery in these tasks, it strengthens your self-confidence and helps you to mature.

What Are the Problems?

The deep and profound feeling of being special that comes with being pregnant often obscures some of the nitty-gritty issues that are bound to come up as your delivery date draws near.

By taking a look at some of the common problems early in your pregnancy, you have more time to prepare for the obstacles ahead. In the last two months of pregnancy, you may feel too heavy and awkward or too easily tired to deal with some of them. It's best to think ahead and plan as soon as possible.

One of the most important problems is *money*. It's a fact that single mothers do not live as well as married mothers, or as women without children. Because so many teenage mothers don't finish high school, have no specific job skills or job experience, and must stay at home to care for their children, a great number of young mothers go on welfare and/or live in poverty.

One study shows that of the mothers who had given birth while still in their teens, and who had kept their babies, 90 percent ultimately used government assistance.

The father of your baby is required by law to help support his child. But payments are usually very small, and most young fathers stop paying after a year or two. It may take a court order to receive payments again. If your boyfriend moves to another state or changes his name, it may be extremely difficult to locate him.

Your parents may be able to help for a while, but as you grow older, you will most likely want to become financially independent. Meanwhile, if you are planning to live at home with your baby, your parents may be eligible for state assistance. Look in Chapter 9 under the section, "Informal Foster Care" to learn more.

Friends and relatives may also help out, but it's best to consider such help as temporary. You probably can't count on it lasting until your baby is grown.

If you are extremely resourceful and hardworking, you may be able to make ends meet. Some young women manage successfully, but for most, the lack of money remains a problem in raising a child alone.

A second major problem facing single mothers is *loneliness*. Some girls believe that a baby will take away the loneliness they already feel, or that the child will become a companion or best friend.

Unfortunately, an infant can't fulfill this expectation. As a child grows, a mother feels a need to be with and talk to people her own age. Often, a teenager feels more lonely and isolated from friends and family after the baby is born.

In addition, because a baby takes up so much time and energy, you may feel confined to the house. Going outdoors will revolve around the baby's schedule of sleeping, eating, and bathing and your schedule of cooking, cleaning, dishwashing, laundry, and other chores. You will not be able to leave the house even when the baby is asleep, since babies should never be left unattended.

Friends, who were always there during your pregnancy, may stop coming around after the baby's birth. Your boyfriend may feel happy about the birth of his baby, but he may not be around to relieve you in caring for the child.

The feeling of isolation and loneliness is even greater when the single mother is faced with making so many important, day-to-day decisions about the baby's health and well being by herself. It helps to have someone to talk to when you are unsure about what to do. Your concerns can be as basic as how to decide what clothing to put on the baby to go outside so that the infant is neither over nor under dressed. Or how to handle and care for a baby with diaper rash, or when a baby is spitting up or vomiting, or when the child is ill.

Furthermore, you have to manage money alone. A perfectly balanced budget can be destroyed by an unexpected illness. You may have to think about finishing school or starting a job. The burden of these decisions is on you. Ultimately, you are the one who is responsible for what happens.

You can help with these problems by developing a network of friends, particularly young women who are also raising babies alone. When you do go out, talk to other young mothers you meet at parks or playgrounds. Keep up friendships you made while you were in a maternity home or taking childbirth classes.

Look in your phone book for "Parents Without Partners." Although most of the members are adult parents, this international organization can help teenagers meet new people, provide them with family education and services, as well as refer them to classes and groups specifically organized for single adolescent mothers. The Y.W.C.A. also has parenting programs for teenagers.

Health is another problem facing the teenage mother and her baby. Since you are probably still growing and developing physically, pregnancy and childbirth put an additional strain on your body. You may need extra rest and nutrition that you might not be able to get once you bring the baby home. See a doctor regularly to make sure you are staying in good physical shape. If you are alone with your baby, it's essential that you stay healthy.

Your baby, too, needs careful medical attention. All babies should be checked periodically by a pediatrician. But because many babies born to teenagers are premature, or have low birth weight, your baby may need extra attention and care. Ask your doctor what your baby needs and follow his or her advice.

A problem that is often difficult to admit or talk about is *child abuse.* Few mothers ever believe that they could abuse a child. Yet many do admit to feelings of rage toward and rejection of their child. Sometimes, these feelings emerge when the mother realizes that the baby won't gratify her needs or solve her problems as she had hoped. If a teenage mother doesn't completely understand what is normal behavior for a child during the many stages of infant and child development, she may become frustrated or angry when the baby doesn't behave or obey as she expects. Difficult living conditions can only complicate and add to her stress. It may be too much to cope with and may result in her striking out at her child. This can end in serious emotional or physical damage for the child.

Help is available. There are child abuse hot lines. Look for a listing in the Yellow Pages under "Child Abuse" or in the White Pages under "Parents Anonymous." A hospital or a mental health organization can either offer help or refer you to someone who can. These groups provide aid to both parent and child. If you sometimes feel out of control, it's important to reach out for help.

A special note: It is a sad and startling fact that teenage mothers commit suicide at a rate seven times higher than girls the same age who do not have children. The demands of raising a child are sometimes more than a young person can bear. Overwhelming disappointment, depression, and despair can result. If you can't go on alone anymore, if you feel your life is hopeless, or if you have thoughts of suicide, get help immediately. Call your doctor or pediatrician. Talk to a counselor or a clergyperson. Call a hot line number. Try looking in the phone directory under "Parental Stress" or a mental health agency. Go to the emergency room of the nearest hospital. You will receive help immediately.

In this section, we have talked about some of the major problems faced by teenage mothers. You may encounter some of them, or others not mentioned here. By knowing in advance what problems you may have to confront, you can prepare to deal with them.

Teenage Mothers Who Succeed

Single, teenage mothers who successfully navigate the twists and turns of parenthood are honest about their motivation to have a baby, have achieved a degree of maturity and independent thinking, and accept the fact that they must assume responsibility for the child. However, they do not do it alone. They still need help.

The most ideal conditions for taking on this task are to have parents who accept their daughter and her decision to have a baby, who provide a home, financial and emotional support, guidance in child care—and at the same time, make it clear that she is responsible for the child, not they.

The parents recognize that the teenager will continue to need parenting herself while she learns how to become a parent, and that she will need time to gain both parenting and other life skills to ultimately care for her child completely by herself.

It helps if the young woman already has many homemaking skills, such as cooking, cleaning, and sewing, and enjoys these activities. The ability to handle money and a budget is also important. The young woman who is very interested in the process of child-rearing and development, who reads books, takes classes, and learns from the experience of others, has a better chance at succeeding.

If you have these ingredients, you may feel secure in your ability to parent a child successfully. After a long, hard look at themselves and their situations, some girls may decide that having a baby isn't right for them at this time, after all. If this is the case with you, you still have other options. Adoption and foster care are open to you. If it is still early in your pregnancy, so is abortion. To learn more, read those chapters in this book.

If you have thoughtfully considered all the options and your motivations, and believe that you are ready for parenthood, keeping your baby and raising it yourself may be right for you.

> *My son was born when I was 16. There was nothing I wanted to do more than raise him. Being a good mother was, and still is, so important to me. I like reading everything I can about child care and I've learned so much. I've also grown up a lot. It wasn't easy, especially at first. But I am lucky to have a mother and father who supported me in my decision. They helped me care for the baby so I could finish high school, and now I'm going to a junior college part-time so I can get a good job. I want to be able to move out of my parents' home and support myself and Timmy when I turn twenty. Raising a child is a big responsibility, but I love doing it.—Michelle, 18.*

In general, teenagers who are the happiest with their decision are those who feel that loving and nurturing a child is a very special calling in life. They take their responsibility seriously. They want to give themselves completely to raising a baby, because it both enriches them and provides a healthy, happy start in the life of another human being. They are also aware of the problems they might face, but feel the benefits outweigh the risks.

If this describes your feelings about yourself, you are on your way to being a successful parent.

ELEVEN

YOUR PREGNANCY

I loved being pregnant. It felt so nice to touch my belly and feel the baby inside. I liked being all plump and round.—Jennifer, 16.

I had mixed feelings about being pregnant. Some days I was happy. Other days, I would feel like crying for no reason at all. Then, as my stomach got bigger, I began to feel awkward. Really unbalanced. My body and my head went through some heavy changes in those nine months.—Melanie, 17.

I didn't think I could handle childbirth. I was terribly afraid of labor pains. But I did it! Now, I'm amazed to think my body could produce a perfect little human being. It's like a miracle.— Tiffany, 15.

Having a Baby

Deciding to continue your pregnancy—whether you ultimately choose marriage, adoption, foster care, or raising the baby yourself—means that many changes will take place in the nine months from conception to childbirth. Most teenagers are concerned about the physical changes that will occur. You may be already asking yourself, "What will I look like? What does it feel like to carry a baby? How can I take care of myself and the baby growing inside of me?"

This chapter discusses the many changes that go on in a woman's body during pregnancy, as well as the special care a teenager needs at this time. First, let's take a look at some of the "feeling" changes that may take place inside of you.

Your emotions may swing up and down. One day you may feel optimistic and confident, the next day you may feel irritable or depressed. Many pregnant women report that they are frequently on the verge of tears.

Pregnant teenagers are often confused by their changing moods. Yet these wide swings are normal for most women during pregnancy, especially in the early months. Hormone levels in your body are changing rapidly, and this can cause your emotions to be unpredictable. You must also deal with a changing body-image, perhaps before you have completely adjusted to the changes in your body which started at puberty. What you think about your body will influence how you feel about your pregnancy as it progresses. Family and personal problems can accentuate these mood swings.

By understanding the elements affecting your emotions during pregnancy, you can gain some control over them. It may also help to share your emotions with others—your parents, boyfriend or husband, or with your doctor, social worker or counselor. Talking to other women who are pregnant can be a sharing experience that helps you feel less alone. Enrolling in a childbirth class can also teach you what to expect during pregnancy, labor, and delivery, as well as provide a setting in which to share your thoughts and feelings.

Getting Ready

The miraculous development from fertilized egg to embryo to fetus and finally to baby takes place in about forty weeks or nine months. You can give your baby a healthy start before it is even born by getting good prenatal (before birth) care.

It is very important to see a doctor as soon as you think you are pregnant. An early appointment with an obstetrician (a doctor who specializes in pregnancy and childbirth) can be the best way to maximize your chances of having a healthy baby.

Unfortunately, most teenagers do not get the health care they need. Too many deny their pregnancy, or are afraid of telling others, or don't know where to go for prenatal care.

Because of the lack of early and regular health care, teenage mothers have a much greater chance of delivering babies with low birth weight or birth defects.

Low birth weight can be associated with mental retardation, birth defects, and other developmental problems. Birth defects include heart conditions, blindness, nervous disorders, breathing problems, mental retardation, or deformed parts of the body. One out of ten babies born to teenagers is threatened by low birth weight. In addition, women under 18 are more likely to deliver prematurely, or suffer stillbirth, especially if they have received no prenatal care. Uncared for teenagers also have a higher incidence of delivery complications or infant and maternal mortality (death).

Yet studies show that with good prenatal care, teenagers can deliver as safely, and produce as healthy babies, as women in their 20s.

You can give yourself and your baby a head start by finding a good obstetrician and hospital. To find an obstetrician and a hospital, contact a health care clinic, or check your telephone directory. If you have a family doctor, he or she can recommend an obstetrician for you. Social service organizations or your school counselor or nurse can also refer you to an obstetrician or recommend a hospital.

Good prenatal care involves regular visits to the doctor. Ideally, the first visit should be two or three weeks after missing your menstrual period. For the next five or six months, the pregnant teenager usually sees her doctor every four weeks. During the sixth and seventh months, visits are scheduled every two or three weeks. In the eighth and ninth months, they are increased to once a week. Your doctor will set up a schedule of appointments that is appropriate to the health care you need.

At your first prenatal checkup, your obstetrician will give you a general physical checkup and ask for the date of your last menstrual period and medical history. You will most likely be tested for venereal disease (even if you are married). Your blood type and Rh factor will be identified. Then the obstetrician will perform an internal pelvic examination in order to determine the size of your uterus.

In addition, your pelvic structure and childbearing organs will be checked at this time. At the end of the examination, your obstetrician will give you an approximate "due date"—the day your baby will most likely be born.

Your obstetrician will also explain to you how to care for yourself. He or she may recommend a special diet for you so that you gain the proper amount of weight and get the nutrition you and the growing baby need. Supplemental vitamins may also be recommended.

Feel free to ask questions during this visit, or at any subsequent visit. Write down your questions in advance, because it is easy to forget them once you are in the doctor's office.

In the months ahead, during the prenatal checkups, your obstetrician will take your blood pressure and carry out other routine tests. He or she will also check the growth of the fetus, its position inside the uterus, and the position of the uterus itself. Later on, the obstetrician will listen to the fetus's heart beats with a stethescope. (Ask your doctor to let you listen, too!)

You will most likely deliver your baby in the hospital with which your obstetrician is affiliated. It's a good idea to visit the hospital well before your due date. You will want to know where the hospital is and how to get there. Most hospitals will allow you to visit the maternity ward and the delivery room. Often a nurse or a hospital staff member will give you a tour, explaining procedures and answering questions.

Find out about registration. There may be many forms to fill out. It will be easier on you if you understand them before you go to the hospital to deliver your baby. Often, a pregnant woman can preregister.

Having a baby is expensive. It can cost from $1,000 to $2,500 and up, depending on the length of your hospital stay, and whether there are complications. You will need to show your doctor and the hospital how you plan to pay. Your parents, boyfriend, or husband may be able to assist you. If they have health insurance, their policies may cover your medical expenses. If not, you should contact a social welfare agency. Anyone under twenty-one is eligible for Medicaid, which pays the doctor or hospital directly for birth expenses. Beginning with the fourth month of pregnancy, you may be eligible for assistance under the Aid to Families with Dependent Children (A.F.D.C.) program. Since it takes at least thirty days to process the forms so that you can begin receiving financial aid, apply as soon as you realize you will need help.

You can make childbirth easier for yourself by learning all you can before your baby is born. Find out if childbirth classes are offered in your area. Many hospitals and health care clinics offer such programs. The Red Cross and Y.W.C.A. also offer classes, or can refer you elsewhere. Often it is possible to bring your mother, a relative, your boyfriend, or your husband to childbirth classes.

There is a great deal that needs to be done to prepare for your baby's birth. If you decide to continue your pregnancy to term, begin now to plan for a healthy nine months.

Eating Right and Feeling Good

Most teenagers want to feel and look as good as possible during pregnancy. For many, a major concern is appearance and weight gain. Like a majority of pregnant women, you are probably wondering, "Will I ever look the same again?"

The body does go through some enormous changes during pregnancy, but most women can regain their figures by eating right and exercising regularly.

A healthy diet is important for you and it's vital to your growing baby. An unborn child is completely dependent upon you to supply the nutrition needed to develop normally. Many studies have proven the direct relationship between the mother's diet and the baby's health. The pregnant woman who eats properly has a higher chance of producing a baby who is physically and mentally normal.

The amount of weight you gain is also important to the development of the fetus. Most doctors agree that a gain of twenty to thirty pounds is desirable for most pregnant women. Caution: Do not go on a diet to lose weight while you are pregnant. Trying to hide a pregnancy by using diet pills or skipping meals can be harmful to a developing fetus.

The weight you gain during pregnancy can be lost easily after birth. In fact, the average woman is about twelve or thirteen pounds lighter one hour after birth and another three to seven pounds lighter by the next day. The remaining weight is usually lost within a few weeks, especially when a woman has been eating properly throughout her pregnancy. Your obstetrician or childbirth class instructor can show you exercises to do before and after birth to tone and shape your figure.

Pregnant teenagers, because they are still developing themselves, need extra nutritional care. What should a young pregnant woman eat and how much? Let's take a look at what many doctors and nutritionists recommend:

Dairy Products—(four or more servings a day)
Choose from: milk, skim milk, buttermilk, ice cream, milkshakes, pudding, cheese, and yogurt.
Meat, Fish, and Eggs—(three or four servings a day)
Choose from: beef, pork, chicken, turkey, liver, fresh fish, tuna, eggs, hamburger, meat loaf, occasionally peanut butter, nuts, peas, and beans.
Fruits and Vegetables—(four servings a day)
Choose from: green and yellow vegetables, especially leafy vegetables, oranges, grapefruit, tomatoes, fruit juice, melon, strawberries, and others.
Breads and Cereals—(four servings a day)
Choose from: cooked cereal, cold cereal, macaroni, spaghetti, noodles, rice, whole wheat bread, corn, tortillas, pancakes, graham crackers, and wheat crackers.

Your obstetrician can further advise you about the particular foods and supplemental vitamins you will need. Many pregnant women find that they feel better by eating five or six small meals a day rather than three large ones.

Good, fresh food can be expensive, especially if you are on a limited budget. If you cannot afford the quality or the amount of food recommended, talk to your doctor, a counselor, or a social worker. You may be eligible for food stamps or the Special Supplemental Food Program for Women, Infants and Children (W.I.C.).

Unfortunately, teenagers often have very poor eating habits. This is one of the reasons for health and developmental problems in babies born to women under twenty.

Avoid junk food—candy, sodas, artificial fruit punches, potato chips, pretzels, spicy or greasy foods and presweetened foods. In addition, stay away from extra salty foods. A developing fetus cannot receive much nutrition from junk food and may not develop properly as a result.

You will feel better, too, during your pregnancy by eating well. Your diet need not be bland. It's OK to have a cheeseburger and a milkshake. A pizza once in a while is perfectly nutritious, especially with extra cheese.

When deciding what to eat, ask yourself, "What should I feed my developing baby?" Some teenage mothers find it helpful to think in terms of feeding a newborn baby. For example, you wouldn't offer an infant potato chips or put soda in a baby bottle. But you would want to nourish a baby with plenty of milk and other wholesome foods.

Along these same lines, you wouldn't want to give an infant a cigarette or pills picked up on the street.

The fetus growing within you is affected by everything you put in your body. Because a developing fetus is so small and vulnerable, it cannot defend itself against harmful agents the way an adult or even a teenager can. In fact, the greatest harm can be done during the third to eighth week of pregnancy—a time when most women don't even know for sure they are pregnant!

This is another reason why teenagers have a greater risk of giving birth to babies with birth defects and/or low birth weight: they aren't careful about what they eat, drink, smoke, or swallow, during pregnancy.

For example, smoking cigarettes can reduce the amount of oxygen going to the fetus, which can lead to low birth weight and the problems associated with it.

Drinking alcohol may also hurt the fetus. Heavy drinking can result in a baby's being born with a serious birth defect called Fetal Alcohol Syndrome. Recent evidence shows that even small amounts of alcohol may hinder brain development, lower intelligence, and even cause mental retardation in a developing baby.

Marijuana and other street drugs can be extremely harmful to the fetus. The damage done can be unpredictable. Many young people mix alcohol and drugs, which is doubly destructive. Remember, what may seem like a pleasurable high to you may be a life-threatening assault on a developing fetus.

Pregnant women who are addicted to drugs, such as speed or heroin, will give birth to babies who are also addicted. These infants will have a much rougher course following birth. They will suffer from withdrawal, in addition to other major health problems.

Prescription drugs can also be harmful to your baby. More and more evidence suggests that few drugs are completely safe to the developing fetus. Even aspirin, laxatives, antacids, cold tablets, and nasal sprays could be hazardous to a developing fetus. In general, it's best not to take anything without first consulting your obstetrician. Taking care of yourself increases your chance of delivering a healthy baby.

What's Happening to Your Body

The Three Trimesters

The most obvious physical change that occurs during pregnancy is the shape of a woman's body. A pregnant woman will notice changes even before her abdomen begins to swell. By learning some of the major developments that will occur in your body, you can understand what's normal, how to make yourself more comfortable, and when you should be concerned about a potential complication.

The nine months of pregnancy are divided in three trimesters, each three months long.

The *first trimester* starts at conception and continues for twelve weeks. Most women realize they are pregnant when they miss a normal menstrual period. During the first trimester, pregnant women may experience many symptoms, including nausea, vomiting, loss of appetite, or increased appetite, the craving for certain foods, or the aversion to other foods. Many women experience breast tenderness and enlargement. The area around the nipples may become darker. Some pregnant women feel minor cramping or heaviness in the pelvic area. Tiredness is another symptom, as is the need to urinate more frequently.

At the time of conception, the fertilized egg begins to divide and travels from the fallopian tube into the uterus. Nine to ten days after fertilization, the tiny ball of cells attaches itself to the uterine lining. As the cells continue to divide and differentiate, the amniotic sac and the placenta form. The amniotic sac is filled with a fluid, which protects the developing fetus. The placenta is a very special organ that transmits oxygen and nutrients from the mother's body to the baby's. The fetus is connected to the placenta by the umbilical cord.

A great deal goes on during the first few weeks of pregnancy. The rudiments of all the major organs form. This includes the brain, heart, and lungs, as well as eyes, ears, and bone tissue. By the ninth week, male or female sex and reproductive organs begin to form. In only twelve weeks, the fetus grows from a single cell that can be seen only with a microscope to about three inches in length and a weight of one ounce.

During the *second trimester,* the pregnant woman's abdomen will begin to swell. By the sixth month, she will look obviously pregnant. Many women say this is the most pleasant trimester of pregnancy. Most of the uncomfortable symptoms, such as nausea, have ended by this time. Other women report an increased feeling of optimism and well-being. Between the eighteenth and twenty-second week, an expectant mother will begin to feel the first movements of the baby within her. She may also notice a thin, yellow discharge from the nipples. This is an indication that the breasts are preparing milk for the baby. Wearing small gauze pads in a bra can help to absorb this discharge. A woman may also notice a straight dark line developing from the navel to the pubic hair. This is perfectly normal, and usually lightens considerably, or disappears completely after the pregnancy has ended. Around the sixth month, she may also experience possible groin pain, as ligaments are stretching, and, possibly, uterine contractions. These are called "Braxton-Hicks" contractions, and are sometimes confused with labor pains. These pains are not regular, and often stop by changing positions: such contractions indicate that the uterus is preparing for childbirth.

Between the eighteenth and twentieth weeks, the fetus's heartbeat can first be heard through a stethoscope. (It can be heard many weeks earlier through a Doppler, or ultrasound, stethoscope.) The bones and all the other organs are continuing to grow and form. The baby's teeth begin to develop in the second trimester. By the twenty-fourth week, the fetus is about twelve to fourteen inches long and weighs approximately one-and-a-half to two pounds.

During the *third trimester,* a pregnant woman's abdomen will grow to its fullest point. Many women report feeling uncomfortable during the last months of pregnancy. They have trouble finding a comfortable sitting or lying position. The weight of the fetus presses on the pelvis and lower back, causing cramping and pain, and the need to urinate frequently recurs. If stretch marks have appeared, they may become more obvious. By the ninth month, women often describe shortness of breath and indigestion, due in part to the increased size of the fetus, which causes greater pressure on many internal organs. Backaches, leg cramps, and aching feet are common in the last month. As the due date approaches, a large number of women experience "Braxton-Hicks" contractions with greater intensity and frequency.

The fetus will be kicking and moving more vigorously now. In fact, many pregnant women have trouble sleeping because the baby's movements keep them awake. Fetal movements should be felt every day by the third trimester. If no movement is felt for over twenty-four hours, a pregnant woman should telephone her doctor. By the last trimester, all of the fetus's organs have already formed. The last few months are crucial, because the organs must now continue to mature and develop in order to be functioning properly at the time of birth. The fetus is also gaining weight and strength. By the end of the ninth month, most babies are about twenty inches long, and weigh between seven and eight pounds.

Most pregnancies progress well and on schedule. Sometimes, though, a complication can occur. Call your doctor or hospital *immediately* if you experience any of the following symptoms:

- Bleeding from the vagina, rectum, nipples, or coughing blood.
- Sudden gush of water from the vagina before the due date.
- Unusual vaginal discharge that burns, itches, is green-yellow in color, or is mixed with blood.
- Pain or burning during urination.
- Marked decrease in the amount of urine passed daily.
- Sudden swelling or puffiness of the feet, ankles, hands, fingers, or face.
- Blurred vision, flashes of light, or dots before the eyes, dizziness, or fainting.
- Chills or fever.
- Severe cramps or pain in the abdomen.
- Continuous, severe, or excessive nausea or vomiting.
- Exposure to venereal disease, German measles, or hepatitis.
- Severe, continuous headache.

These symptoms may be caused by a pregnancy disorder, and may result in miscarriage.

Approximately 13 percent of teenage pregnancies are reported to end in miscarriages. A miscarriage is a spontaneous or natural abortion of the embryo or fetus. About one-third of these occur so early in the pregnancy that a young woman may know only that her period was late, and that the flow was heavier than usual.

The cause of miscarriage is unknown in the majority of cases. Among the reasons thought to cause an embryo or fetus to be expelled are malformed or undeveloped childbearing organs, the failure of the embryo to attach itself properly to the uterine wall, infections, and certain drugs. It is believed that genetic abnormality and/or an abnormal fertilized egg is responsible for most miscarriages.

Be aware of any potentially dangerous symptoms. Most times, a pregnant teenager can continue normally with her life, especially early in her pregnancy.

Education need not be interrupted. Some schools have special classes or courses for pregnant teenagers. Your school counselor may be able to provide you with information about other educational programs in your area. Continuing school, or getting a job, often helps young women feel better about themselves.

Light exercise is important, too. Walking is about the best exercise possible for a pregnant woman. Your obstetrician or childbirth class instructor may show you some special exercises to do to help make the delivery easier.

Strenuous activity, such as jogging, dancing, tennis, skating, swimming, and contact sports, may need to be restricted during your pregnancy. Ask your obstetrician to what degree you can continue these sports.

Many women wonder about sex during pregnancy. Most doctors agree that sexual intercourse early in the pregnancy is not harmful to the fetus, but some may recommend abstinence during the last six to eight weeks. Ask your obstetrician what is best for you.

Pregnant teenagers should sleep eight to ten hours a night, and take a short nap once during the day. Prop up your legs whenever you can, to relieve pressure and to improve blood circulation.

Wear sturdy, comfortable shoes with a low heel. High heels can cause increased back pain and poor posture, as well as leg and foot cramps during pregnancy. As you get larger, your balance may be a little off. Wearing high heels, loose sandals, or floppy slippers can cause you to trip and fall.

As your breasts enlarge, you will need a well-fitting bra that gives support to the breasts. Avoid wearing anything tight or restrictive, especially around the abdomen and legs.

Wear loose-fitting outfits. Many teenagers dislike wearing maternity clothes, because they look "dumpy" or out of fashion. There is no need to dress very differently from other people your age. Many styles today are suitable for wear whether or not you are pregnant. You can even find designer jeans with an elastic panel for your growing abdomen.

You can take showers or baths. Wash your breasts carefully. Some doctors recommend that you avoid soap around the nipples that can dry and remove natural oils. Pregnancy affects your scalp and hair, too. You may find that you need to shampoo and condition your hair more often.

You can learn more about the three trimesters and how to care for yourself by asking your obstetrician, taking childbirth classes, and reading books about pregnancy.

Labor and Childbirth

The questions most asked by teenagers are: "How will I know when it's time?" "How long will it last?" and "How much will it hurt?"

To answer the first question, birth occurs mostly within two weeks of the due date. There are several signs that indicate labor will begin soon.

The first sign can occur as early as one month before the baby is born. Near the end of your pregnancy, you may notice that you are carrying the baby lower than before. This is because the fetus has slowly "dropped" into the pelvic area, preparing itself for birth. This is called "engagement" or "lightening." Usually this occurs ten to fourteen days before labor begins.

Yet another sign that labor will begin shortly is discharge of mucus from the vagina that is pink or red in color, or is streaked with blood. This is called "show," or "losing the mucus plug." This signals that the cervix is beginning to open.

Still another sure sign is the "breaking of waters," or "rupture of the membranes." When this occurs, there is a gush of water from the vagina. Contractions may have already begun, or will usually begin six to forty-eight hours later.

The most well known sign that labor has begun is "contractions" or "labor pains." Contractions may feel like menstrual cramps, and they can be mild to moderate to strong. The contractions may be accompanied by low backache or a feeling of intense pressure in the abdomen. They become regular, get stronger and closer together as time passes. First contractions are usually fifteen to thirty minutes apart and last thirty to forty-five seconds. As labor progresses, the contractions come closer together and last sixty to ninety seconds. Labor pains, however, are different for each woman. Be aware of the changes that are occurring in your body. They indicate that the process of childbirth is beginning.

It's time to call the obstetrician or hospital when the contractions are strong, regular, and three to five minutes apart, or if the bag of waters breaks (breaking of waters), whether or not contractions have started.

The length of labor is different for each woman, but on the average, first-birth labor takes about fourteen hours.

No one can predict the amount of pain you will feel. Each woman has a different tolerance for pain. At any point during labor and childbirth, if the pain becomes too intense, analgesics or anesthesia may be given to ease the discomfort. Many women receive local anesthesia to block certain nerves so that the pain will be reduced in that area. Most obstetricians avoid using general anesthesia, because it interferes with the baby's first breathing.

There are three stages of labor, beginning with the dilation of the cervix, progressing to the birth of the baby, and ending with the delivery of the placenta (afterbirth).

The *first stage* begins with regular contractions of the uterus, which open the cervix so that the baby can pass through the vagina, or birth canal. During early labor, the cervix progressively thins (effacement) and begins opening (dilating) to four centimeters (a centimeter is equal to .39 inches). Many women recall feeling excited, nervous, and energetic during this period.

As labor progresses, contractions come closer together and become more intense as the cervix opens from four to eight centimeters (cm.). This is often called "active labor." There is more pain, cramping, and pressure. A laboring woman becomes very concentrated at this time, directing all her energy to the act of childbirth.

"Hard labor," or "transition," occurs when the cervix opens from eight to ten cm. During this time, contractions are very strong and seem continuous. Many feel panicky, frustrated, or want to quit at this point. There is more pain than before. Often, a woman will have leg cramps or uncontrollable shaking. Many feel hot during contractions and cold in between. There is a strong urge to bear down and help push out the baby. If the bag of waters has not yet broken, it most likely will during hard labor. This is the most difficult time of labor. Although the last few centimeters of dilation can occur quite rapidly, it usually takes about one hour in an average first birth.

When the cervix has dilated, or opened, sufficiently, the *second stage*—when the baby travels down the birth canal and is born—can now take place. This takes anywhere from one minute to several hours. There is a feeling of great pressure in the vagina and rectum. The urge to push is stronger. As the baby passes through the birth canal, a woman may experience a renewed sense of energy. And when the baby is born, there is an enormous feeling of relief, exhilaration, exhaustion, or many emotions released together all at once. Many women cry.

> *It was incredible. My mom was with me and we both cried when the baby was finally born.—Jody, 19.*

During the *third stage,* the placenta and other membranes pass out of the vagina. This can take from two to twenty minutes after birth.

Sometimes, a small incision (an episiotomy) is done on the perineum (lower surface of the vaginal opening) to allow the baby's head to emerge without causing a laceration (tearing of tissue) to occur. You should discuss the possibility of these procedures with your doctor before the due date.

On occasion, complications can arise. By receiving early and regular prenatal care, many potential problems can be detected and special measures put into effect at the time of delivery. Sometimes, complications occur unexpectedly during labor. Caesarean delivery, known as C-section (an incision made through the abdominal wall and uterus in order to remove the baby), may be necessary. The doctor will monitor the progress of your labor and advise you if this is indicated.

After You've Given Birth

Each woman experiences birth in her own way. The circumstances surrounding the birth of your baby will influence your feelings afterward, as will the final outcome of your pregnancy—marriage, adoption, foster care, or keeping the baby.

Many young women are happy and excited that they were able to give birth to a healthy baby. For some, childbirth represents the high point of nine months of planning for and fantasizing about the baby. Others feel pride and confidence in themselves for having accomplished a very difficult task.

When labor has been very painful, women can also feel angry or treated unfairly because no one prepared them for the experience. Other young women feel betrayed by the lack of control they have over their bodies during childbirth. Still others may feel even more isolated from, and abandoned by, family or a boyfriend who did not support their decision to carry the baby to term.

In the weeks to come, your body will go through the process of returning to normal. This is called the postpartum period, which lasts from six to eight weeks. The uterus returns to its original size in about six weeks. During the first few days, you will experience menstrual-like cramping. For several weeks, you will have a vaginal discharge called "lochia." At first, the flow is heavy and bright red in color. After a few days, the flow lessens and changes to a reddish-brown color. In about a week, the color will go from a light brown or pink to almost clear. Gradually, it decreases and stops altogether in about three to four weeks. Wear sanitary napkins. Tampons should not be inserted for at least two weeks after childbirth.

Menstruation will begin in about six to eight weeks. The first few periods after childbirth are usually heavier and last longer than average. It may take several months for the menstrual cycle to regulate itself as it was before pregnancy. Breast feeding may delay the start of menstruation.

Following childbirth, your breasts will begin to produce "colostrum," a thin, bluish milk, rich in protective antibodies, which protects your baby from various infections. On the third day, the breasts suddenly become full and firm. Now, the nipple produces a bluish-white milk, and after another day or so, a thick yellow-white milk. If you are planning to breast feed, speak to your doctor about what is involved.

If you do not plan to breast feed, your obstetrician can prescribe an injection or pills to stop the flow of milk. Wearing a supportive bra, using an ice pack on your breasts and taking aspirin will ease some of the breast discomfort until milk production stops entirely.

Many young women are released from the hospital after a few days. Follow your obstetrician's instructions for aftercare and proper diet. Also inquire when you can go back to school or work.

You may wonder when you can begin sexual intercourse again. Generally, most doctors advise a young woman to wait at least until the six-week checkup, or until after her menstrual period starts again.

Since you can become pregnant again before your next period if you have unprotected intercourse, you may want to discuss birth control methods with your doctor or counselor. Contrary to popular myth, it *is* possible to get pregnant even while breast feeding. Discuss with your doctor which birth control method will meet your special needs.

Many women report feeling sad, "blue," or tearful a few days after giving birth. It can last anywhere from a few days to a few weeks. It does not occur in every woman, but if it happens to you, it's helpful to know that it's to be expected and temporary.

The hormone levels in your body change rapidly after birth and contribute to this "down" feeling. In addition, a lot of women are also overwhelmed by the responsibility and the amount of work involved once they are home with the baby. If this depressed feeling lasts for more than a few weeks, seek professional counseling.

If you are keeping your baby, it will be important to have help at home at this time. This should be arranged in advance. It will be extremely difficult to care for the baby alone while you are still recovering from the effects of childbirth and regaining your strength.

Even though you are still a teenager, childbirth separates you in significant ways from other teens. You have had an "adult" experience which will most likely deepen and broaden your understanding of yourself and others.

Whatever the outcome of your pregnancy (adoption, foster care, or raising the baby yourself), there will be a period of adjustment. Read the chapters on these options for more information.

TWELVE

THE FUTURE— GOING ON FROM HERE

Getting pregnant changed my life. I never thought about the future. I just figured there'd always be someone to take care of me if something went wrong. Now I know I've got to take care of myself. I guess that's a part of becoming an adult.—Joyce, 16.

I had a baby four months ago and I think I'm pregnant again. I don't know what I'm going to do. Maybe I'd better start getting some control over my life.—Jessie, 15.

My boyfriend and I thought sex was just fun and fooling around. After I got pregnant, we realized it's a lot more serious than that. We're careful about birth control now. And you know what? Our relationship has gotten a lot deeper. It's like we're taking care of each other now.— Melissa, 17.

A Child No More

Everyone, at some time in life, has an experience of such significance that it changes them, perhaps dramatically. Pregnancy may have been that kind of experience for you. In a very short period of time, you found out you were pregnant, made a decision about the outcome of your pregnancy, and carried it out.

Like you, many teenagers go through this process. Some continue their pregnancy and ultimately choose marriage, or adoption, or raising the baby as a single mother. Others choose to end the pregnancy by having an abortion. For a few, the pregnancy ends in miscarriage. No matter what the outcome of your pregnancy, changes have undoubtedly occurred in your life. Even if you thought you were pregnant but found out were not this time, the reality of that possibility can change the way you think about yourself and your future.

One of the major changes occurs when a teenager comes to terms with the fact that she no longer has the body of a child, but that of a woman. In very down-to-earth terms, this means that every time you have sexual intercourse, there is the possibility that you will get pregnant—every time, for approximately the next thirty to thirty-five years.

Your body has a special rhythm that you will become more aware of as you grow older. The beautiful and complicated process that goes on within it, resulting in your monthly menstrual period, will continue for most of your life. You are fertile—that is, your ovaries release an egg each month. If you have unprotected intercourse when the egg is present, you will get pregnant. Furthermore, you can never be absolutely sure when the egg is present. It is very important that you make the connection between sexual intercourse and pregnancy.

However mixed your feelings about your pregnancy have been, you have learned what many women do not find out until much later in life:

   —that you can get pregnant very easily, and
   —you don't have to.

In other words, you have a choice, one that no one else can make for you. Choosing to protect yourself means taking responsibility for being sexual and taking control of this part of your life.

If the experience of being pregnant has made you feel that you are too young to handle all the physical and emotional consequences of sex, you may decide to wait until you are older, or until you are married, before you have sexual intercourse again.

If you feel that you will continue to be sexually active, and you do not want to get pregnant, there are ways to prevent it. You can choose a method of birth control and use it properly and consistently.

Pregnant Again . . . ?

Unfortunately, many teenagers do get pregnant again, often after only a few months. Three-fifths of all teenage pregnancies are second pregnancies.

There are several reasons why so many young women find themselves pregnant again.

The first has to do with the complex feelings and motivation of a girl who wants to have a baby. Sometimes, she could not keep the baby the first time she got pregnant. Perhaps her parents were against it, or her boyfriend abandoned her. Or she had no means to keep the baby and raise it herself, so her pregnancy resulted unwillingly in abortion or adoption. Yet, for some of the reasons discussed in Chapter 1, she wants a baby desperately. So she gets pregnant again, hoping "this time it will be different." Each time, she faces the same roadblocks, the same inner and outer conflicts that have not been resolved and that prevent her from keeping the baby she wants. Such a young woman puts herself through the same physical and emotional agony each time. It is just as difficult to give up the baby a second time as it is the first.

This pattern of behavior often continues until a girl is able to take positive steps to understand and make peace with her mixed feelings, steps that help her to stop trying to get her emotional needs met in ways that only end in pain and disappointment. When this happens, she is on the way to taking control of her life.

> *I'm pretty unhappy about a lot of things in my life. Getting pregnant twice was part of that. But something good came of it. I met a counselor who talked to me and really listened. She got me involved with a youth group that meets once a week. That's helping me to slowly sort*

*out my life. I'm beginning to understand why I
do the things I do, and like myself as I am.—
Nicole, 15.*

A second reason for repeated pregnancies is the denial of sexuality. There are many teenagers who, even after getting pregnant, find it hard to admit to themselves that they have sexual feelings and experiences. These are often young women who have the idea that sex is "bad" or "wrong," and who are getting little or no pleasure from the act of sexual intercourse. They are usually doing it to gain acceptance and affection from a boyfriend.

These are young women who have not yet come to terms with the conflict they have between the need to be sexual and their need to feel good about themselves. For them, these two needs cannot be met at the same time. Being sexual does not make them feel good about themselves. When they get pregnant, they feel they have gotten the punishment they deserve and are paying for their "mistake." This "atonement" helps them to feel good about themselves again. The result is, they do not prepare for sex because they tell themselves it cannot happen again. When it does happen again, the whole cycle repeats itself.

Melissa, 17, began to think more seriously about her sexual feelings after she became pregnant. She has been telling her girlfriends:

> *Hey, this is not something that will go away.
> You can't escape it. You can't ignore it. You can't
> put your head in the sand and say, "It won't
> happen to me." You have to deal with sex or it
> will deal with you when you get pregnant.*

Melissa is learning to accept her sexuality. She has asked her boyfriend to use condoms, even though at first he was against it. She said she'd rather risk losing him than getting pregnant again.

This brings us to a third reason. Many teenagers get pregnant again because they find the idea of birth control distasteful or frightening.

It's unnatural—putting chemicals like pills or foam in your body. And things like diaphragms are just gross.—Danielle, 14.

Many girls feel extremely uncomfortable about touching their genitals in order to use foam or a diaphragm. An I.U.D. seems terrifying to many teenagers (although they are rarely prescribed for women who have not given birth). The Pill has some side effects associated with it and many myths. In reality, dangerous side effects from the Pill are extremely rare in young women. Often the Pill is simply not practical for the teenager who has sex only once in a while. Too many young men don't—or won't—wear condoms, either because they are unprepared for sexual activity themselves, are too embarrassed to purchase condoms, or think birth control is the girl's responsibility.

Frequently, birth control is not used by teenagers because of the way sexual intercourse happens. It is often hurried, done in places that don't provide privacy or time to use many of the effective methods. Mostly, birth control is not used because the passionate feelings are so urgent young people don't want to interrupt their lovemaking, or they are not comfortable enough with sex or each other to discuss it beforehand.

Many women overcome their negative feelings about birth control at the time of an unplanned pregnancy, because they do not want to become pregnant again and realize they don't have to. They come to terms with their sexuality and accept their womanly bodies. Talking to a counselor might help you. She may suggest a method with which you can feel comfortable and which suits your needs. For more information, visit a family planning clinic and read books about contraception.

If you are keeping the child, whether you are married or single, it is important to consider the benefits of spacing births apart by two or three years. It is better for your health, and, with babies born several years apart, there is a lower risk of premature birth and birth defects.

Discuss birth control with your partner. Although only the

woman carries a pregnancy within her body, *couples* get pregnant together. Therefore, *couples* need to share the responsibility for the outcome of sexual intercourse.

There are many girls who decide they will not have sexual intercourse again until they are older or married. They make a firm decision and stick to it. They learn that it's "OK" to say "no." They spend the rest of their teen years developing other parts of their lives.

With abstinence, there are no risks. It is a 100 percent effective method of birth control. It also eliminates the worry of contracting a venereal disease, such as herpes, gonorrhea, or syphilis. The risk of VD increases with the number of sexual partners you have. Several studies, too, have linked cervical cancer with early sexual activity and multiple partners.

When making a decision to abstain, you must be honest with yourself. Though negative feelings about sex can be strong following an unplanned pregnancy, sexual expression is a part of being human, and sexual feelings may resurface sometime in the future. Prepare yourself for this possibility and recognize it. If you feel that you are going to be sexually active again and do not want to get pregnant, use a contraceptive.

Going On from Here

Getting pregnant is a milestone experience in every young woman's life. For some, the outcome is positive in that they were able to end a pregnancy they were unprepared for, or they were able to continue a pregnancy they wanted. There were painful moments for many. For a few, the experience was devastating.

No matter what the outcome of your pregnancy, your life continues to move forward. How you deal with the future will depend on how you feel about yourself and your experience.

It is important to keep in mind that you have been through a deeply human experience—one that may have left you both stronger and more vulnerable. Stronger, because it took courage to carry out your decision—whether it was for abortion, adoption, getting married, or raising the child yourself. More vulnerable, because you may have come face-to-face with yourself and your feelings for the first time.

If you are feeling regretful or ashamed, it is important to be generous toward, and forgiving of, yourself. Life has many difficult and painful experiences—experiences that help us learn that neither we, nor others, are perfect. That realization can help us to be more accepting of ourselves and more compassionate and understanding of others. Value the experience. It is part of who you are.

Remember that you are a unique and valuable person, with a potential you have only begun to use. Your whole life is ahead of you. There will be many choices to make in the future. You now have some experience in making hard decisions and carrying them out.

Becoming an adult woman takes time and many life experiences. Pregnancy is only one of them—one that has come early in your life, perhaps before you felt ready for it. Yet you have had to meet the challenge of dealing with a very real situation that could not be wished away. Making a decision and carrying it out shows that you are taking responsibility for your life. This is the first step to adulthood.

Unplanned pregnancy can be a crisis, but a crisis is also an opportunity for growth. Coping successfully with crisis builds confidence, and confidence gives you the ability to test yourself and grow. Growth leads to maturity.

Sex and pregnancy are experiences that carry profound responsibilities. It's early to learn this. But if the experience of pregnancy can be used to gain this knowledge, to learn how to make important decisions about your life, and to achieve independence and responsibility, then you have indeed matured tremendously. You have successfully navigated a rugged course and are approaching the shores of adulthood.

A Special Word for Parents

Mom, I'm Pregnant was written primarily for teenagers, but as our title suggests, it was also written for mom, the person to whom most girls turn when they are in trouble. The majority of girls do tell their mothers, and usually their fathers as well, if they are faced with the crisis of an unexpected pregnancy. It is a situation that is taking place in households across America, crossing all economic and ethnic groups. It is an experience most parents hope will not happen to them or to their daughters, yet, the possibility is very real indeed.

Over three-fourths of teenage girls gain sexual experience before they reach the age of twenty. Most are unmarried. The possibility of pregnancy exists for all these young women and, directly or indirectly, affects the lives of millions of parents every year. Our first chapter, "You're Not Alone," applies to parents as well.

Many parents react with shock and disbelief to the news that their daughter is pregnant. Some feel anger, hurt, and deep disappointment. As we discuss in Chapter 4, your daughter's pregnancy can suddenly confront you with the realization that she's not a little girl anymore. She is no longer a child but a sexually active young woman who is growing away from her parents and establishing new, intimate relationships outside the family.

The years of adolescence are a time of separation for parent and child. Communication often breaks down, especially about such deeply personal subjects as love, passion, sexual pleasure, birth control, and pregnancy. It is often as difficult for adults to share this intimate part of their lives with their children as it is for teenagers to reveal their private feelings to their parents.

159

Many times, family relationships go through turbulent changes as the teenager struggles between her need to be independent and her need to be taken care of.

One mother of a 15-year-old teenager told us, "I don't understand my daughter. One day she wants me to buy her a skateboard, the next day she tells me she's pregnant. Then she decides she wants to keep the baby and be a mother. And now, she clings to me like a little girl wanting reassurance. How can I help her? I don't know where to begin."

Teenage pregnancy is often a cry for help, a plea for love, an appeal to be taken care of again.

Yet, most parents don't know what to do when their daughter comes home and says, "Mom, I'm pregnant." Suddenly, they are thrown into a situation for which they are not prepared. Parents need answers to very concrete questions: "Where can our daughter get a pregnancy test? Is abortion safe for her? How will her health and her development be affected if she carries the child to term? Should she marry the boy? What about adoption? Who can we talk to? What are the laws? What are our rights? How will this affect her life and her future?"

This book provides the facts for both teenagers and parents, as well as information about where to go for further help. It also can serve as a guideline for parents to help them understand their daughter's emotional and physical needs during this time. Every parent of a pregnant girl should also become aware of warning signs that may require immediate medical attention. These, too, are listed in this book.

We encourage teens to share the knowledge of their pregnancy and to discuss its outcome with their parents. Experience has shown that parental support can be immeasurably valuable. It is our hope that this book can help to open the doors of communication between you and your daughter. Talking and listening are the keys to a closer relationship and to a healthy adjustment to the final decision about the pregnancy.

We hope that this book will be read by adolescents and parents *before* pregnancy occurs. Teenage girls can benefit by reading about other girls' experiences. One teen we interviewed said, "I wish I had known what was involved before getting pregnant. The decisions you have to make are so hard. No one prepared me for the physical pain and the emotional hurt I went through. I just wasn't old enough to handle it alone."

Sharing this book with your daughter can help her establish the very real connection between "going all the way" and getting pregnant.

In conclusion, our underlying theme throughout this book is "growing up"—that is, achieving self-knowledge and independence, as well as accepting responsibility. Unplanned pregnancy can be a crisis that interferes with this development. Even so, with help, a teenager can use this experience to grow and mature.

We hope that with your love and guidance, your daughter can come through this difficult period in her life with increased confidence in herself and renewed hope for her future.

Where to Go for Help

A Guide to Hot Lines and Agencies in the United States and Canada

If you think you are pregnant, it's important to get help as soon as possible. The agencies listed in this chapter are there to assist you. They can help you get a pregnancy test, provide counseling services and birth control information, and aid you in carrying out your decision concerning the outcome of your pregnancy.

Many of these agencies have branch offices which may be more conveniently located. Make a long distance phone call if you need to. The agency you contact may be able to refer you to a clinic or hospital near you.

There are many other clinics and organizations to help teenagers, in addition to the ones listed in this book. If you do not see one in or near your home town, call one of the agencies listed and ask to be referred to the one nearest you. Or check your telephone directory (under "Abortion," "Adoption Agencies," "Birth Control," "Clergy," "Clinics," "Counseling" or "Counselors," "Government Offices," "Human Services," "Marriage," "Pregnancy," "Religious Organizations," "Social Service Organizations," and "Welfare Organizations"). You might also go to your local library and ask for the telephone directory of the largest town or city near you.

Hot Lines
National hot lines have an 800 prefix and are toll free (there is no charge). Local hot lines are indicated with an asterisk (*).

163

Abortion Assistance Association	800/523-5101
Abortion Information Bureau, Inc.	800/523-5350
Abortion Information Service	800/321-1682
Central Florida Women's Health Organization	800/221-2568
Family Health Services	800/682-5229—in Mississippi
Hope Clinic for Women	800/682-3121—in Illinois 800/851-3130—in Missouri
Indianapolis Women's Center	800/382-9029
Jacksonville Women's Health Organization, Inc.	800/221-2568
National Abortion Federation	800/223-0618
National Operation Venus Hotline	800/523-1885 800/462-4966—in Philadelphia
National Runaway Switchboard	800/621-4000 800/972-6004—in Illinois
National Women's Health Organization, Inc.	800/221-2568
New England Women's Service	800/682-9218—in Massachusetts
Parents Anonymous	800/421-0353 800/352-0386—in California
Southern Women's Service	800/922-9750—in South Carolina
Tampa Women's Health Center	800/282-0743
Westchester Women's Health Organization	800/221-2568
Women for Women of Cincinnati	800/582-7388—in Ohio 800/543-7213—in Indiana, Kentucky, and West Virginia
Women's Health Center, Inc.	800/432-8517

The United States

ALABAMA

Family and Child Services
5201 Airport Highway
Birmingham, Alabama 35222
205/592-2630

Planned Parenthood of Alabama
1108 South 20th Street
Birmingham, Alabama 35256
205/933-8444

The Salvation Army Maternity
  Home
6001 Crestwood Boulevard
Birmingham, Alabama 35212
205/595-8343

Family Services Center
316 Longwood Drive
Huntsville, Alabama 35801
205/539-5717

Planned Parenthood Association
  of Madison County
125 Earl Street
Huntsville, Alabama 35805
205/539-2746

Family Counseling Center
6 South Florida Street
Mobile, Alabama 36606
205/471-3466

Beacon Clinic
1011 Monticello Court
Montgomery, Alabama 36117
205/277-6212

Family Guidance Center
925 Forest Avenue
Montgomery, Alabama 36106
205/262-6669

ALASKA

Booth Memorial Home
3600 East 20th Avenue
Anchorage, Alaska 99501
907/279-0522

Planned Parenthood of Alaska
2820 C Street
Anchorage, Alaska 99503
907/279-2576

*Youth Services Center Crisis
  Line
Anchorage, Alaska
907/279-9154

ARIZONA

Florence Crittenton Services
P.O. Box 5216
Phoenix, Arizona 85010
602/271-9116

Planned Parenthood of Central
  and Northern Arizona
1301 South Seventh Avenue
Phoenix, Arizona 85007
602/257-1515

Catalina Family Planning
5700 East Pima Street
Tucson, Arizona 85712
602/296-6116

Department of Pediatrics
University of Arizona
College of Medicine
Tucson, Arizona 85724
602/882-6173

Planned Parenthood of Southern
   Arizona
127 South Fifth Avenue
Tucson, Arizona 85701
602/624-1761 or 602/624-7477

ARKANSAS

Florence Crittenton Home
   Services
3600 West 11th Street
Little Rock, Arkansas 72204
501/663-3129 or 501/663-1244

Little Rock Pregnancy
   Counseling Service
5512 West Markham Street
Little Rock, Arkansas 72205
501/661-9230

Family Service Agency of Central
   Arkansas
North Little Rock Community
   Center Bldg.
P.O. Box 500
North Little Rock, Arkansas
   72115
501/758-1516

Planned Parenthood of Eastern
   Oklahoma and Western
   Arkansas
1007 South Peoria
Tulsa, Oklahoma 74120
918/587-1101

CALIFORNIA

Alameda Family Service Agency
746 Eagle Avenue
Alameda, California 94501
415/521-4151

*Helpline Youth Counseling
Bellflower, California
213/920-1706

*Berkeley Youth Alternatives
Berkeley, California
415/849-1402

Family Service Agency of San
   Mateo County
1870 El Camino Real
Burlingame, California 94010
415/692-0555

Adolescent Clinic
Naval Regional Medical Center
Camp Pendleton, California
   92055
714/725-5556

*Youth Emergency Assistance
Chula Vista, California
714/422-9294

Planned Parenthood Association
   of Yolo County
116 B Street
Davis, California 95616
916/758-4592

Planned Parenthood of
   Humboldt County
2316 Harrison Avenue
Eureka, California 95501
707/442-5709

Adolescent Clinic
Valley Medical Center
445 South Cedar
Fresno, California 93702
209/251-4833

Planned Parenthood of Fresno
633 North Van Ness
Fresno, California 93728
209/486-2411

Florence Crittenton Services of
    Orange County, Inc.
P.O. Box 447
Fullerton, California 92632
714/870-5522

*Odyssey Crisis Line
Fullerton, California
714/871-9365

*Western Youth Services
Fullerton, California
714/871-5646

Glendale Family Service
    Association
3435 North Verdugo Road
Glendale, California 91208
213/248-2286

West Coast Medical Group
426 East 99th Street
Inglewood, California 90301
213/674-5971

Booth Memorial Home and Day
    Care Center
2670 Griffin Avenue
Los Angeles, California 90031
213/225-1586

Department of Pediatrics
Division of Adolescent Medicine
Children's Hospital of Los
    Angeles
4650 Sunset Boulevard
Los Angeles, California 90027
213/660-2450

Family Service of Los Angeles
1521 Wilshire Boulevard
Los Angeles, California 90017
213/484-2944

Los Angeles Florence Crittenton
    Services
234 Avenue 33
Los Angeles, California 90031
213/225-4211

Planned Parenthood-World
    Population
3100 West Eighth Street
Los Angeles, California 90005
213/380-9300

Planned Parenthood of Monterey
    County
5 Via Joaquin
Monterey, California 93940
408/373-1691

Booth Memorial Home and Day
    Care Center
2794 Garden Street
Oakland, California 94601
415/532-3345

Family Service Association of the
    Mid-Peninsula
375 Cambridge Avenue
Palo Alto, California 94306
415/326-6576

Pasadena Planned Parenthood
1045 North Lake Avenue
Pasadena, California 91104
213/794-5737

Every Woman's Clinic
1936 Linda Drive
Pleasant Hill, California 95423
415/825-7900

Family Service of Pomona Valley
2055 North Garey Avenue
Pomona, California 91767
714/593-7408

Human Concern Foundation
Concern Health Center
3610 Central Avenue
Riverside, California 92506
714/682-4400

*Youth Service Center
Riverside, California
714/683-5193

Family Service Agency of the
  Greater Sacramento Area
709 21st Street
Sacramento, California 95814
916/448-8284

Planned Parenthood Association
1507 21st Street
Sacramento, California 95814
916/446-5034

Family Service Agency
1669 North E Street
San Bernardino, California 92405
714/886-6737

Department of Pediatrics
Adolescent Clinic
Naval Regional Medical Center
San Diego, California 92134
714/233-2722

Door of Hope Home
2799 Health Center Drive
San Diego, California 92123
714/279-1100

Family Service Association of San
  Diego County
7645 Family Circle
San Diego, California 92111
714/279-0400

Planned Parenthood of San
  Diego County
2100 Fifth Avenue
San Diego, California 92101
714/231-1282

Children's Hospital of San
  Francisco
3700 California Street
San Francisco, California 94119
415/387-8700

Family Service Agency of San
  Francisco
1010 Gough Street
San Francisco, California 94109
415/474-7310

Florence Crittenton Services
840 Broderick Street
San Francisco, California 94115
415/567-2357

Planned Parenthood of Alameda-
San Francisco
1660 Bush Street
San Francisco, California 94109
415/441-5454

University of California Medical
Center
Adolescent Clinic
400 Parnassus Avenue
San Francisco, California 94143
415/524-1485

Planned Parenthood Association
17 North San Pedro
San Jose, California 95110
408/287-7526 or 408/287-7532

Planned Parenthood Association
2211-2215 Palm Avenue
San Mateo, California 94403
415/574-2622

Planned Parenthood Association
20 H Street
San Rafael, California 94901
415/454-0471

Planned Parenthood Association
1901 North Broadway
Santa Ana, California 92706
714/973-1727

*Crisis Line
Santa Barbara, California
805/569-2255

Family Service Agency of Santa
Barbara
800 Santa Barbara Street
Santa Barbara, California 93101
805/965-1001

Planned Parenthood of Santa
Barbara County
518 Garden Street
Santa Barbara, California 93101
805/963-5801

Planned Parenthood of Santa
Cruz County
212 Laurel Street
Santa Cruz, California 95060
408/426-5550

Family Service Association of the
Rio Hondo Area
Santa Fe Springs, California
90670
213/949-9691

The Woman's Health Care
Project
1711 Ocean Park Boulevard
Santa Monica, California 90405
213/450-2191

*Youth Services Crisis Line
South Lake Tahoe, California
916/541-8500

Stanford University Medical
Center
Stanford, California 94305
415/935-3010

Planned Parenthood of San
Joaquin County
19 North Pilgrim Street
Stockton, California 95205
209/466-2081

Stockton Pregnancy Control
Medical Clinic
4545 Georgetown Plaza E25
Stockton, California 95207
209/951-5655

Family Planning Alternatives,
Inc.
505 West Olive Avenue
Sunnyvale, California 94305
408/739-5151

Family Service Association of
Orange County
17421 Irvine Boulevard
Tustin, California 92680
714/838-7377

Planned Parenthood of Contra
Costa
1291 Oakland Boulevard
Walnut Creek, California 94596
415/935-3010

COLORADO

Rocky Mountain Planned
Parenthood
1537 Alton Street
Aurora, Colorado 80010
303/360-0006

Boulder Planned Parenthood
4500 North Broadway
Boulder, Colorado 80302
303/447-1040

Colorado Springs Planned
Parenthood
1619 West Colorado Avenue
Colorado Springs, Colorado
80904
303/475-7162

Women's Health Service Clinic
111 East Dale
Colorado Springs, Colorado
80903
303/471-9492

Denver Chapter, Planned
Parenthood
2030 East Twentieth Avenue
Denver, Colorado 80205
303/388-4777

Human Services, Inc.
838 Grant Street
Denver, Colorado 80203
303/830-2714

Larimer County Planned
Parenthood
149 West Oak Street
Fort Collins, Colorado 80521
303/456-0517

Pueblo Planned Parenthood
151 Central Main
Pueblo, Colorado 81003
303/545-0246

CONNECTICUT

Planned Parenthood League of
Connecticut
1067 Park Avenue
Bridgeport, Connecticut 06604
203/366-0664

Planned Parenthood League of
Connecticut
44 Main Street
Danbury, Connecticut 06810
203/743-2446

Division of Child and Adolescent
  Behavior
University of Connecticut,
  Department of Pediatrics
Mount Sinai Hospital
500 Blue Hills Avenue
Hartford, Connecticut 06107
203/242-4431

Planned Parenthood League of
  Connecticut
297 Farmington Avenue
Hartford, Connecticut 06105
205/522-6201

Planned Parenthood League of
  Connecticut
45 Broad Street
Middletown, Connecticut 06457
203/347-5255

Family Counseling of Greater
  New Haven
One State Street
New Haven, Connecticut 06511
203/865-1125

Jewish Family Service of New
  Haven
152 Temple Street
New Haven, Connecticut 06510
203/777-6641

Planned Parenthood League of
  Connecticut
129 Whitney Avenue
New Haven, Connecticut 06510
203/865-0595

Family Service Association of
  Southern New London County
11 Granite Street
New London, Connecticut 06320
203/442-4319

Planned Parenthood League of
  Connecticut
420 Williams Street
New London, Connecticut 06320
203/443-5820

Family and Children's Services
60 Palmer's Hill Road
Stamford, Connecticut 06902
203/324-3167

Planned Parenthood League of
  Connecticut
80 Lincoln Avenue
Stamford, Connecticut 06902
203/327-2722

Planned Parenthood League of
  Connecticut
27 Pearl Street
Torrington, Connecticut 06790
203/489-5500

Planned Parenthood League of
  Connecticut
125 Grove Street
Waterbury, Connecticut 06702
203/753-2110

Jewish Family Service of Greater
  Hartford
740 North Main Street
West Hartford, Connecticut 06117
203/236-1927

*Perception House
Willimantic, Connecticut
203/423-7731

Planned Parenthood League of
  Connecticut
791 Main Street
Willimantic, Connecticut 06226
203/423-8426

DELAWARE

Delaware League of Planned
  Parenthood
825 Washington Street
Wilmington, Delaware 19801
302/655-7293

Family Service of Northern
  Delaware
809 Washington Street
Wilmington, Delaware 19801
302/654-5303

DISTRICT OF COLUMBIA

Adolescent Clinic
Walter Reed Army Medical
  Center
Washington, D.C. 20012
202/576-2051

Adolescent Medicine
Children's Hospital of District of
  Columbia
2125 Thirteenth Street, N.W.
Washington, D.C. 20009
202/835-4352

Adolescent Medicine Clinic
Howard University Hospital
2041 Georgia Avenue, N.W.
Washington, D.C. 20060
202/745-1592

Division of Adolescent Medicine
Department of Pediatrics
Georgetown University Medical
  Center
3800 Reservoir Road
Washington, D.C. 20007
202/625-7383

Family and Child Services of
  Washington
929 L Street, N.W.
Washington, D.C. 20001
202/289-1510

The Florence Crittenton Home
4759 Reservoir Road, N.W.
Washington, D.C. 20007
202/333-3600

New Summit Medical Center
2520 L Street, N.W.
Washington, D.C. 20037
202/337-7200

Planned Parenthood of
  Metropolitan Washington,
  D.C.
1108 16th Street, N.W.
Washington, D.C. 20036
202/347-8500

Preterm
1990 M Street, N.W.
Washington, D.C. 20036
202/452-8400

Women's Clinic-Washington
  Hospital Center
110 Irving Street, N.W.
Washington, D.C. 20010
202/541-6037

FLORIDA

Planned Parenthood of South
  Palm Beach & Broward
  Counties
160 N.W. 4th Street
Boca Raton, Florida 33432
305/368-1023

Family Counseling Center
2960 Roosevelt Boulevard
Clearwater, Florida 33520
813/536-9427

Planned Parenthood Association
  of Greater Miami
351 Altara Avenue
Coral Gables, Florida 33146
305/443-0774

*Youth Alternatives Crisis Line
Daytona Beach, Florida
904/252-6550

Family Service Agency
1300 South Andrews Avenue
Fort Lauderdale, Florida 33335
305/524-8286

Planned Parenthood of North
  Central Florida
P.O. Box 12385
Gainesville, Florida 32604
904/377-0881

The Buckner Manor
P.O. Box 5616
Jacksonville, Florida 32207
904/398-3265

Family Consultation Service of
  Jacksonville and Duvall
  County
1639 Atlantic Boulevard
Jacksonville, Florida 32207
904/396-4846

*Jacksonville Youth Center
Jacksonville, Florida
904/725-6662

Planned Parenthood of Northeast
  Florida
828 San Marco Boulevard
Jacksonville, Florida 32207
904/398-2618

Planned Parenthood of Central
  Florida
1104 North Dakota Avenue
Lakeland, Florida 33805
813/688-2646

Jewish Family and Children's
  Service
1709 S.W. 27th Street
Miami, Florida 33145
305/445-0555

United Family and Children's
  Service
2190 N.W. Seventh Street
Miami, Florida 33125
305/643-5700

Planned Parenthood-Naples
Center
482 Tamiami Trail North
Naples, Florida 33579
813/262-0301

Central Florida Women's Health
Organization, Inc.
609 East Colonial Drive
Orlando, Florida 32803
305/898-0921

Women's Awareness
3690 N.E. Third Avenue
Pompano Beach, Florida 33064
305/946-0400

Family Counseling Center of
Brevard
220 Coral Sands Drive
Rockledge, Florida 32955
305/632-5792

Family Counseling Center of
Sarasota County
3205 South Gate Circle
Sarasota, Florida 33579
813/955-7017

Planned Parenthood of
Southwest Florida
1958 Prospect Street
Sarasota, Florida 33579
813/953-4060

Family Service Association of
Greater Tampa
205 West Brorein Street
Tampa, Florida 33606
813/251-8477

GEORGIA

Atlanta Center for Reproductive
Health
1285 Peachtree Street, N.E.
Atlanta, Georgia 30309
404/892-8608

The Bridge Crisis Line
Atlanta, Georgia
404/881-8344

Child Service and Family
Counseling Center
1105 Peachtree Street, N.E.
Atlanta, Georgia 30357
404/873-6916

Midtown Hospital
144 Ponce de Leon Avenue
Atlanta, Georgia 30308
404/875-3411

Planned Parenthood Association
of Atlanta Area, Inc.
15 Peachtree Street, N.E.
Atlanta, Georgia 30303
404/688-9300

Planned Parenthood of East
Central Georgia, Inc.
1289 Broad Street
Augusta, Georgia 30902
404/724-5557

Family Counseling Center
102 Seventh Street
Columbus, Georgia 31902
404/327-3238

Family Counseling Center of
  Macon and Bibb County
830 Mulberry Street
Macon, Georgia 31201
912/745-2811

Family Counseling Center of
  Savannah
428 Bull Street
Savannah, Georgia 31401
912/233-5729

HAWAII

Child and Family Service
200 North Vineyard Boulevard
Honolulu, Hawaii 96817
808/521-2377

Hawaii Planned Parenthood, Inc.
1164 Bishop Street
Honolulu, Hawaii 96813
808/521-6991

Honolulu Booth Memorial
  Services for Young Women
2950 Manca Road
Honolulu, Hawaii 96822
808/988-7423

IDAHO

Booth Memorial Home and Day
  Care Center
1617 North 24th Street
Boise, Idaho 83702
208/343-3571

Planned Parenthood Association
  of Idaho
214 East Jefferson Street
Boise, Idaho 83702
208/345-0760

ILLINOIS

Family Service and Visiting Nurse
  Association of the Alton-Wood
  River Region
211 East Broadway
Alton, Illinois 62002
618/463-5959

Family Counseling Center
5109 North Illinois Street
Belleville, Illinois 62221
618/235-5656

*Youth in Crisis Hotline
Berwyn, Illinois
312/484-7400

Family Counseling Center
201 East Grove Street
Bloomington, Illinois 61701
309/828-4343

Planned Parenthood of Mid
  Central Illinois, Inc.
201 East Grove Street
Bloomington, Illinois 61701
309/827-8025

Planned Parenthood of
  Champaign County
314 South Neil Street
Champaign, Illinois 61820
312/359-8022

Family Service of Champaign
  County
608 West Green, Urbana
Champaign-Urbana, Illinois
  61801
217/384-1911

Adolescent Clinic
Rush-Presbyterian Hospital
1753 West Congress Parkway
Chicago, Illinois 60612
312/942-5000

American Red Cross Disaster and
    Family Service
43 East Ohio Street
Chicago, Illinois 60611
312/440-2000

Booth Memorial Hospital
5040 North Pulaski Road
Chicago, Illinois 60630
312/725-7441

Jewish Family and
Community Service
One South Franklin Street
Chicago, Illinois 60606
312/346-6700

*New Life House
Chicago, Illinois
312/271-6165

Planned Parenthood
    Association—Chicago Area
55 East Jackson Boulevard
Chicago, Illinois 60604
312/322-4200

United Charities of Chicago
14 East Jackson Boulevard
Chicago, Illinois 60604
312/461-0800

Planned Parenthood of Decatur
988-990 South Main Street
Decatur, Illinois 62521
217/429-9211

Family Service Association of
    Greater Elgin Area
165 Division Street
Elgin, Illinois 60120
312/695-3680

Hope Clinic for Women, Ltd.
1602 21st Street
Granite City, Illinois 62040
618/451-5722

*Aunt Martha's Youth Service
    Center
Park Forest, Illinois
312/747-2701

Counseling and Family Service
1821 North Knoxville Avenue
Peoria, Illinois 61603
309/685-5287

Planned Parenthood Association
    of Peoria Area
530 Fulton Street
Peoria, Illinois 61602
309/673-0907

Northern Illinois Women's Center
2500 North Rockton Avenue
Rockford, Illinois 61103
815/963-4101

Family Service Center of
    Sangamon County
1308 South Seventh Street
Springfield, Illinois 62703
217/528-8406

Planned Parenthood-Springfield
  Area
500 East Capitol
Springfield, Illinois 62701
217/544-2744

INDIANA

Planned Parenthood of South
  Central Indiana
421 South College Avenue
Bloomington, Indiana 47401
812/336-0219

Family Counseling Service of
  Elkhart County
101 East Hively Avenue
Elkhart, Indiana 46517
219/295-6596

Family and Children's Services
305 South Third Avenue
Evansville, Indiana 47708
812/425-5181

Planned Parenthood of
  Southwestern Indiana
1610 South Weinbach Avenue
Evansville, Indiana 47714
812/479-1466

*Youth Service Bureau Crisis
  Line
Evansville, Indiana
812/425-4355

Family and Children's Services
2712 South Calhoun
Fort Wayne, Indiana 46907
219/744-4326

Lutheran Social Services
330 Madison Street
Fort Wayne, Indiana 46802
219/426-3347

Planned Parenthood of
  Northeastern Indiana
347 West Berry
Fort Wayne, Indiana 46802
219/423-1322

Family Service Association
615 North Alabama Street
Indianapolis, Indiana 46204
317/634-6341

Indianapolis Women's Center
5626 East 16th Street
Indianapolis, Indiana 46218
317-353-9371

Jewish Family and Children's
  Services
1717 West 86th Street
Indianapolis, Indiana 46260
317/872-6641

Planned Parenthood Association
  of Indianapolis, Inc.
615 North Alabama Street
Indianapolis, Indiana 46204
317/637-8230

*Stopover Crisis Line
Indianapolis, Indiana
317-635-9301

Family Service Agency of
  Tippecanoe County
225 North Fourth Street
Lafayette, Indiana 47901
317/423-5361

Tecumseh Area Planned
  Parenthood
1016 East Main
Lafayette, Indiana 47902
317/742-9073

Planned Parenthood of
  Northwest Indiana, Inc.
8645 Connecticut
Merrillville, Indiana 46410
219/769-3500

Family and Children's Center
1411 Lincoln Way
Mishawaka, Indiana 46544
219/259-5666

*Crisis Intervention Center
Muncie, Indiana
317/289-0404

Family Services of Delaware
  County
615 East Washington Street
Muncie, Indiana 47305
317/284-7789

Planned Parenthood of East
  Central Indiana, Inc.
110 North Cerry at West Main
Muncie, Indiana 47305
317/282-3546

Planned Parenthood of North
  Central Indiana
201 South Chapin
South Bend, Indiana 46625
219/289-7062

Women's Pavilion of South Bend,
  Inc.
425 North St. Louis Street
South Bend, Indiana 46617
219/234-0071

Family Service Association in
  Terre Haute
619 Cherry Street
Terre Haute, Indiana 47807
812/232-4349

Planned Parenthood Association
  of Wabash Valley
330 South Street
Terre Haute, Indiana 47808
812/238-2636 or 812/232-0183

IOWA

*Shelter House Crisis Line
Ames, Iowa
515/233-2330

Planned Parenthood of Des
  Moines County
610 North Fourth
Burlington, Iowa 52601
319/753-2281

Planned Parenthood of Southeast
  Iowa
403 Tama Building
Burlington, Iowa 52601
319/753-6209

Family Service Agency
400 Third Avenue, S.E.
Cedar Rapids, Iowa 52401
319/398-3574

Planned Parenthood of Linn
  County
1500 Second Avenue, S.E.
Cedar Rapids, Iowa 52403
319/363-8572

Family and Children's Service of
  Davenport
115 West Sixth Street
Davenport, Iowa 52803
319/323-1852

Family Counseling Center
1321 Walnut
Des Moines, Iowa 50309
515/288-9020

Planned Parenthood of Mid-Iowa
P.O. Box 4557
Des Moines, Iowa 50306
515/280-7000

Planned Parenthood of North Lee
  County
631 Avenue H
Fort Madison, Iowa 52627
319/372-1130

Adolescent Medicine
Departments of
  Medicine/Pediatrics
University of Iowa Hospitals
Iowa City, Iowa 52240
319/356-3447

Planned Parenthood of South Lee
  County
127 South Tenth
Keokuk, Iowa 52632
319/524-2759

Planned Parenthood of Henry
  County
125½ West Monroe
Mt. Pleasant, Iowa 52641
319/385-4310

Family Service Center
2601 Douglas Street
Sioux City, Iowa 51104
712/277-4031

Florence Crittenton Home
1105 28th Street
Sioux City, Iowa 51104
712/255-4321

Planned Parenthood Committee
  of Sioux City
2831 Douglas Street
Sioux City, Iowa 51104
712/277-3332

Family Service League
2530 University Avenue
Waterloo, Iowa 50701
319/235-6271

KANSAS

Hays Planned Parenthood
115 East Sixth
Hays, Kansas 67601
913/628-2434

Family and Children's Service
5424 State Avenue
Kansas City, Kansas 66102
913/287-1300

Booth Memorial Residence
2050 West 11th Street
Wichita, Kansas 67201
316/263-6174

Family Planning Alternatives
518 East Pine Street
Wichita, Kansas 67214
316/264-0611

Planned Parenthood of Kansas
2226 East Central
Wichita, Kansas 67214
316/263-7575

KENTUCKY

Mountain Maternal Health
  League
P.O. Box 429
Berea, Kentucky 40403
606/986-4677

Family Counseling Service
620 Euclid Avenue
Lexington, Kentucky 40502
606/266-0425

Lexington Planned Parenthood
  Center
508 West Second Street
Lexington, Kentucky 40507
606/252-8494

Division of Adolescent Medicine
Department of Pediatrics
Children's Hospital
University of Louisville
Louisville, Kentucky 40206
502/584-2471

Family and Children's Agency
1115 Garvin Place
Louisville, Kentucky 40201
502/583-1741

Planned Parenthood of Louisville
834 East Broadway
Louisville, Kentucky 40204
502/584-2471

LOUISIANA

Family Counseling Agency
301 Fourth Street
Alexandria, Louisiana 71301
318/448-0284

Family Counseling Service
544 Colonial Drive
Baton Rouge, Louisiana 70806
504/926-5083

Metairie Women's Medical
  Center
3008 19th Street
Metairie, Louisiana 70002
504/835-2842

Family Service Society
535 Gravier Street
New Orleans, Louisiana 70130
504/524-7471

*The Greenhouse Crisis Line
New Orleans, Louisiana
504/944-2477

MAINE

Community Counseling Center
622 Congress Street
Portland, Maine 04101
774-5727

MARYLAND

Family and Children's Society
204 West Lanvale Street
Baltimore, Maryland 21217
301/669-9000

Florence Crittenton Services of
  Baltimore, Inc.
3110 Crittenton Place
Baltimore, Maryland 21211
301/366-4333

Jewish Family and Children's
  Services
5750 Park Heights Avenue
Baltimore, Maryland 21215
301/466-9200

Planned Parenthood Association
  of Maryland
610 North Howard Street
Baltimore, Maryland 21201
301/752-0131

*Grassroots Crisis Line
Columbia, Maryland
301/531-6677

Family Service of Montgomery
  County
One West Deer Park Road
Gaithersburg, Maryland 20877
301/840-2000

Gynecare Center
Suite 714, Empire Towers
7300 Ritchie Highway
Glen Burnie, Maryland 21061
301/761-4774

Family Service Agency/Big
  Sisters of Washington County
138 East Antietam Street
Hagerstown, Maryland 21740
301/733-5858

Hagerstown Reproductive Health
  Services
100 West Washington Street, #302
Hagerstown, Maryland 21740
301/733-2400

*Second Mile House Crisis Line
Hyattsville, Maryland
301/927-1386

Planned Parenthood of Prince
  George County
Landover Mall, East Tower
  Building, #203
Landover, Maryland 20785
301/773-5601

Family Service of Prince George's
  County
7580 Annapolis Road
Lanham, Maryland 20801
301/459-2121

Planned Parenthood of
  Metropolitan Washington,
  D.C.
Randolpf Medical Center
4701 Randolpf Road
Rockville, Maryland 20852
301/468-7676

Adolescent Clinic
Montgomery County Health
  Department
8500 Colesville Road
Silver Spring, Maryland 20910
301/587-4565

Maryland Children's and Family Services
303 West Chesapeake Avenue
Towson, Maryland 21204
301/825-3700

MASSACHUSETTS

*Project Rap Crisis Line
Beverly, Massachusetts
617/922-0000 or 617/927-4506

*The Bridge Crisis Line
Boston, Massachusetts
617/227-7114

Charles Circle Clinic
711 Boylston Street
Boston, Massachusetts 02116
617/723-5400

Crittenton Hastings House of the Florence Crittenton League
10 Perthshire Road
Boston, Massachusetts 02135
617/782-7600

Family Service Association of Greater Boston
34½ Beacon Street
Boston, Massachusetts 02108
617/523-6400

*Project Place Crisis Line
Boston, Massachusetts
617/262-3740

New England Women's Service
1031 Beacon Street
Brookline, Massachusetts 02146
617/738-1370

Preterm, Inc.
1842 Beacon Street
Brookline, Massachusetts 02146
617/738-6210

Cambridge Family and Children's Service
99 Bishop Richard Allen Drive
Cambridge, Massachusetts 02139
617/876-4210

Concord Family Service Society
Community Agencies Building
Concord, Massachusetts 01742
617/369-4909

Family Service of Dedham
18 Norfolk Street
Dedham, Massachusetts 02026
617/326-0400

Family Service Association
101 Rock Street
Fall River, Massachusetts 02720
617/678-7541

Children's Aid and Family Service
47 Holt Street
Fitchburg, Massachusetts 01420
617/345-4147

Cape Cod Family and Children's Service
175 West Main Street
Hyannis, Massachusetts 02601
617/775-8605

Family Service Association of Greater Lawrence
430 North Canal Street
Lawrence, Massachusetts 01840
617/683-9505

Florence Crittenton League, Inc.
201 Thorndike Street
Lowell, Massachusetts 01852
617/452-9671

Jewish Family Service of the
  North Shore
564 Loring Avenue
Salem, Massachusetts 01970
617/745-9760 or 617/745-9761

*Crisis Center, Inc.
Worcester, Massachusetts
617/791-6562

Family Service Organization of
  Worcester
31 Harvard Street
Worcester, Massachusetts 01609
617/756-4646

Jewish Family Service of
  Worcester
646 Salisbury Street
Worcester, Massachusetts 01609
617/755-3101

MICHIGAN

Child and Family Services of
  Washtenaw
2301 Platt Road
Ann Arbor, Michigan 48104
313/971-6520

Washtenaw County League for
  Planned Parenthood
912 North Main Street
Ann Arbor, Michigan 48104
313/996-4000

*Other Room Crisis Line
Bay City, Michigan
517/895-8532

Planned Parenthood Association
  of Southwestern Michigan
785 Pipestone
Benton Harbor, Michigan 49022
616/925-1306

Mecosta County Family Planning
P.O. Box 1156
Big Rapids, Michigan 49307
616/796-8644

Ambulatory Adolescent Service
Children's Hospital of Michigan
James Couseum Clinic
Detroit Medical Center
Detroit, Michigan 48201
313/494-5050

Booth Memorial Hospital
130 West Grand Boulevard
Detroit, Michigan 48216
313/496-1500

Catholic Social Services of Wayne
  County
9851 Hamilton Avenue
Detroit, Michigan 48202
313/883-2100

*Crisis Line
Detroit, Michigan
313/873-0678

Family Service of Detroit and
  Wayne County
51 West Warren Avenue
Detroit, Michigan 48201
313/833-3733

Family Trouble Clinic
11000 West McNichols
Detroit, Michigan
313/862-0330

Lula Belle Stewart Center
1534 Webb Avenue
Detroit, Michigan 48206
313/867-2372

Planned Parenthood League, Inc.
13100 Puritan
Detroit, Michigan 48227
313/861-6704

Family Service Agency of
  Genesee County
202 East Boulevard Drive
Flint, Michigan 48503
313/767-4014

Flint Community Planned
  Parenthood Association
310 East Third Street, YWCA
Flint, Michigan 48503
313/238-3631

*The Bridge Crisis Line
Grand Rapids, Michigan
616/451-3001

Family Service Association of
  Kent County
1122 Leonard, N.E.
Grand Rapids, Michigan 49503
616/774-0633

Planned Parenthood Centers of
  West Michigan
425 Cerry, S.E.
Grand Rapids, Michigan 49503
616/774-7005

Salvation Army Genesis House
1215 East Fulton
Grand Rapids, Michigan 49503
616/409-9468

Planned Parenthood of Ionia
  County
111 Kidd Street
Ionia, Michigan 48846
616/527-3250

Family Service and Children's Aid
  of Jackson County
729 West Michigan Avenue
Jackson, Michigan 49204
517/782-8191

Reproductive Health Care Center
  of South Central Michigan
4201 West Michigan Avenue
Kalamazoo, Michigan 49005
616/372-1200

Womancare of Lansing
3401 East Saginaw, #107
Lansing, Michigan 48912
517/337-7350

Marquette-Alger Planned
  Parenthood
228 West Washington
Marquette, Michigan 49855
906/225-5070

Family Aid and Family Service of
  Macomb County
57 Church Street
Mount Clemens, Michigan 48043
313/468-2656

Muskegon Area Planned
  Parenthood Association, Inc.
1642 Peck
Muskegon, Michigan 49441
616/722-2928

Shiawassee County Planned
  Parenthood Association
826 West King
Owosso, Michigan 48867
517/723-6420

Northern Michigan Planned
  Parenthood Association
820 Arlington
Petoskey, Michigan 49770
616/347-9692

*The Sanctuary Crisis Line
Pleasant Ridge, Michigan
313/547-2260

Family and Children Services of
  Oakland
50 Wayne Street
Pontiac Michigan 48058
313/332-8352

Northland Family Planning
  Clinic, Inc., West
10,000 Wayne Road
Romulus, Michigan 48174
313/941-1810

Catholic Social Services
1424 East Eleven Mile Road
Royal Oak, Michigan 48067
313/548-4044

*Interlink Crisis Line
Saginaw, Michigan
517/753-3431

Jewish Family Service
24123 Greenfield
Southfield, Michigan 48075
313/559-1500

Northland Family Planning Clinic
One Northland Plaza;
Suite 1104
20755 Greenfield
Southfield, Michigan 48075
313/559-0590

*Link Crisis Intervention Center
St. Joseph, Michigan
616/983-6351

MINNESOTA

Central Minnesota Planned
  Parenthood
507 Washington
Brainerd, Minnesota 56401
218/722-0833

Family Service of Duluth
600 Ordean Building
424 Superior Street
Duluth, Minnesota 55802
218/722-7766

Planned Parenthood of Northeast
  Minnesota
211 West Second
Duluth, Minnesota 55802
218/722-0833

Planned Parenthood of Northeast
  Minnesota
211 West Second
Mankato, Minnesota 56001
507/378-5581

Family and Children's Service
414 South Eighth Street
Minneapolis, Minnesota 55404
612/340-7444

Meadowbrook Women's Clinic
6490 Excelsior Boulevard
Minneapolis, Minnesota 55426
612/925-4640

Midwest Health Center for
  Women
825 South 8th Street
Minneapolis, Minnesota 55404
612/332-2311

Planned Parenthood of
  Metropolitan Minneapolis
127 South Tenth Street
Minneapolis, Minnesota 55403
612/332-8931

Planned Parenthood of Rochester
  Area
3½ South Broadway
Rochester, Minnesota 55901
507/288-5186

Family Service of Greater St.
  Paul
333 On-Sibley Street
St. Paul, Minnesota 55101
612/222-0311

Planned Parenthood of
  Minnesota
1965 Ford Parkway
St. Paul, Minnesota 55116
612/698-2401 or 612/646-9603

Planned Parenthood of St. Paul
  Metropolitan Area
110 Hamm Building
408 St. Peter Street
St. Paul, Minnesota 55102
612/224-1361

Planned Parenthood of Western
  Minnesota
Bonde Building
Fourth Street & Litchfield
  Avenue
Willmar, Minnesota 56201
612/235-9150

MISSISSIPPI

Gulf Coast Family Counseling
  Agency
1718 West Howard Avenue
Biloxi, Mississippi 39530
601/435-4581

Delta Women's Clinic East, Inc.
1319 24th Avenue
Gulfport, Mississippi 39501
601/864-4840

Family Health Services
2906 North State Street
Dale Building; Suite 501
Jackson, Mississippi 39216
601/981-3010

Family Service Association of
    Greater Jackson
1510 North State Street
Jackson, Mississippi 39202
601/353-3891

Mississippi Children's Home
    Society
P.O. Box 1078
Jackson, Mississippi 39205
601/352-7784

MISSOURI

Contraceptive Counseling Service
3394 McKelvey Road
Bridgeton, Missouri 63044
314/739-6499

Planned Parenthood of Central
    Missouri
800 North Providence Road
Columbia, Missouri 65201
314/449-2475

Adolescent Clinic
Children's Mercy Hospital
240 Sillham Road
Kansas City, Missouri 64108
816/234-3000 or 816/234-3050

Broadway Women's Center, Inc.
4400 Broadway
Kansas City, Missouri 64111
816/561-4400

Crittenton Center
10918 Elm Avenue
Kansas City, Missouri 64134
816/765-6600

Family and Children Services of
    Kansas City
3515 Broadway
Kansas City, Missouri 64111
816/753-5280

Jewish Family and Children
    Services
1115 East 65th Street
Kansas City, Missouri 64131
816/333-1172

Planned Parenthood Association
    of Western Missouri/Kansas
1001 East 47th Street
Kansas City, Missouri 64110
816/756-2277

Planned Parenthood of Northeast
    Missouri
P.O. Box 763
Kirksville, Missouri 63501
816/665-5674

Planned Parenthood of the
    Central Ozarks
Box 359; 1032B Kings Highway
Rolla, Missouri 65401
314/364-1509

The Greater Springfield Planned
    Parenthood Association, Inc.
1918 East Meadowmere
Springfield, Missouri 65804
417/869-6471

Catholic Family Service
4140 Lindell Boulevard
St. Louis, Missouri 63108
314/371-4980

Family and Children's Service of
 Greater St. Louis
2650 Olive Street
St. Louis, Missouri 63103
314/371-6500

Family Guidance Center
200 Corby Building
5th & Felix
St. Joseph, Missouri 64501
816/364-1501

Jewish Family and Children's
 Service
9385 Olive Boulevard
St. Louis, Missouri 63132
314/993-1000

Lutheran Family and Children's
 Services
4625 Lindell Boulevard
St. Louis, Missouri 63108
314/361-2121

Planned Parenthood Association
 of St. Louis
2202 South Hanley Road
St. Louis, Missouri 63144
314/781-3800

Reproductive Health Services
100 North Euclid, Suite 203
St. Louis, Missouri 63108
314/367-0300

*Youth in Need Crisis Line
St. Charles, Missouri
314/724-7171

*Youth Emergency Service
University City, Missouri
314/727-6294

MONTANA

Planned Parenthood of Billings
2722 Montana Avenue
Billings, Montana 59101
406/248-3636

Blue Mountain Women's Clinic
515 Kensington; Suite 24A
Missoula, Montana 59801
406/542-0029

Planned Parenthood of Northern
 Rockies
P.O. Box 4047
Missoula, Montana 59806
406/728-0702

NEBRASKA

*Crisis Line
Lincoln, Nebraska
401/475-6261

Family Service Association of
 Lincoln
1133 H Street
Lincoln, Nebraska 68508
402/476-3327

Planned Parenthood of Lincoln
3830 Adams Street
Lincoln, Nebraska 68504
402/467-4691

Booth Residence and Emergency
 Lodge
426 South 40th Street
Omaha, Nebraska 68131
402/344-7000

Family Service
2240 Landon Court
Omaha, Nebraska 68102
402/345-9118

Planned Parenthood of Omaha
4610 Dodge
Omaha, Nebraska 68132
402/554-1045

NEVADA

*Focus Crisis Line
Las Vegas, Nevada
702/384-2914

Planned Parenthood of Southern
  Nevada, Inc.
601 South 13th Street
Las Vegas, Nevada 89101
702/385-3451

Planned Parenthood of Northern
  Nevada, Inc.
455 West Fifth Street
Reno, Nevada 89503
702/329-1781

West End Women's Group of
  Reno
601 Mill Street
Reno, Nevada 89502
702/329-0616

NEW HAMPSHIRE

Planned Parenthood Association
  of the Upper Valley
127 Mascoma Street
Lebanon, New Hampshire 03766
603/448-1214

NEW JERSEY

Planned Parenthood—Greater
  Camden Area
590 Benson Street
Camden, New Jersey 08103
609/365-3519

Jewish Family Service of
  Southern New Jersey
100 Park Boulevard
Cherry Hill, New Jersey 08002
609/662-8611

Metropolitan Medical Associates,
  Inc.
40 Engle Street
Englewood, New Jersey 07631
201/567-0522

Family Counseling Service
10 Banta Place
Hackensack, New Jersey 07601
201/342-9200

Jewish Family Service
20 Banta Place
Hackensack, New Jersey 07601
201/488-8340

Planned Parenthood Center of
  Bergen County
575 Main Street
Hackensack, New Jersey 07601
201/489-1140

Family Service Association of
  Middlesex County
901 Raritan Avenue
Highland Park, New Jersey 08904
201/572-0300

New Jersey Gynecological
  Associates
22 Ball Street
Irvington, New Jersey 07111
201/373-2600

Adolescent Services and Clinic
Morristown Memorial Hospital
Morristown, New Jersey
201/540-5199

Family Service of Morris County
62 Elm Street
Morristown, New Jersey 07960
201/538-5260

Planned Parenthood of
  Northwest New Jersey, Inc.
197 Speedwell Avenue
Morristown, New Jersey 07960
201/539-9580

Planned Parenthood League of
  Middlesex County
211 Livingston Avenue
New Brunswick, New Jersey
  08901
201/246-2411

Department of Pediatrics
New Jersey Medical School
Martland Hospital
65 Bergen Street
Newark, New Jersey 07107
201/456-5481

Family Service Bureau of Newark
15 Fulton Street
Newark, New Jersey 07102
201/624-0913

Planned Parenthood-Essex
  County
151 Washington Street
Newark, New Jersey 07102
201/622-3900

*Operation Junction Line
North Wildwood, New Jersey
609/729-1663

Nutley Family Service Bureau
155 Chestnut Street
Nutley, New Jersey 07110
201/667-1884

Passaic County Planned
  Parenthood Center
175 Market Street
Paterson, New Jersey 07505
201/345-3883

Planned Parenthood of Union
  County Area, Inc.
234 Park Avenue
Plainfield, New Jersey 07060
201/756-3736

Family Service Agency of
  Princeton
120 John Street
Princeton, New Jersey 08540
609/924-2098

Planned Parenthood of
  Monmouth County, Inc.
69 Newman Springs Road
Shrewsbury, New Jersey 07701
201/842-9300

Family Service Association of
  Summit
43 Franklin Place
Summit, New Jersey 07901
201/273-1414

Family Service Association
143 East State Street, M-5
Trenton, New Jersey 08608
609/393-1626

Jewish Family Service of Greater
  Mercer County
51 Walter Street
Trenton, New Jersey 08628
609/882-9317

Planned Parenthood Association
  of the Mercer Area
437 East State Street
Trenton, New Jersey 08608
609/599-3736 or 609/599-4881

Jewish Family Service of North
  Jersey
One Pike Drive
Wayne, New Jersey 07470
201/595-0111

Family Service Association of
  Atlantic County
4000 Black Horse Pike
West Atlantic City, New Jersey
  08232
609/645-2942

NEW MEXICO

Abortion and Pregnancy Testing
  Clinic
107 Girard Boulevard, S.E.
Albuquerque, New Mexico 87106
505/265-9511

Family Counseling Service
4011 Silver Avenue, S.E.
Albuquerque, New Mexico 87108
505/265-8596

Rio Grande Planned Parenthood
113 Montclaire, S.E.
Albuquerque, New Mexico 87108
505/265-5976

Planned Parenthood of South
  Central New Mexico
302 West Griggs Avenue
Las Cruces, New Mexico 88001
505/524-8516

Planned Parenthood of
  Southwest Mexico
110 East 11th
Silver City, New Mexico 88061
505/388-1553

NEW YORK

Family and Children's Service of
  Albany
12 South Lake Avenue
Albany, New York 12203
518/462-6531

*REFER Crisis Line
Albany, New York
518/434-1202

Upper Hudson Planned
  Parenthood, Inc.
259 Lark Street
Albany, New York 12210
518/434-2182

Planned Parenthood of Broome
and Chenango Counties, Inc.
710 O'Neill Building
Binghamton, New York 13901
607/723-8306

Division of Adolescent Medicine
Montefiore Hospital and Medical
Center
111 East 210th Street
Bronx, New York 10467
212/920-4045

Comprehensive Adolescent
Medical Program
Brookdale Hospital Medical Cntr.
Linden Boulevard-Rockaway
Parkway at Brookdale Plaza
Brooklyn, New York 11212
212/240-5077

Midwood Adolescent Project
1484 Flatbush Avenue
Brooklyn, New York
212/434-4458

Women's Medical Services at
Kingsbrook
Rutland Road & East 49th Street
Brooklyn, New York 11203
212/756-8438

Adolescent Unit
Roswell Park Memorial Institute
Buffalo, New York 14263
716/845-4406

Child and Family Services
330 Delaware Avenue
Buffalo, New York 14202
716/842-2750

*Compass House Crisis Line
Buffalo, New York
716/886-0935

Planned Parenthood Center of
Buffalo
210 Franklin Street
Buffalo, New York 14202
716/853-1771

Planned Parenthood of the
Southern Tier, Inc.
200 East Market Street
Elmira, New York 14901
607/734-3313

Planned Parenthood of the Finger
Lakes, Inc.
435 Exchange Street
Geneva, New York 14456
315/781-1092

Southern Adirondack Planned
Parenthood
144 Ridge Street
Glen Falls, New York 12801
518/798-8999

Planned Parenthood of Suffolk
County
17 East Carver Street
Huntington, New York 11743
516/427-7154

Planned Parenthood of Tompkins
County
314 West State Street
Ithaca, New York 14850
607/273-8325

Planned Parenthood of Nassau
County
107 Mineola Boulevard
Mineola, New York 11501
516/724-0144

Planned Parenthood of Orange-
Sullivan, Inc.
91 DuBois Street
Newburgh, New York 12550
914/562-5748

Adolescent Health Center
Mt. Sinai Hospital
19 East 101st Street
New York, New York 10029
212/650-6016 or 650-5892

Center for Reproductive and
Sexual Health
424 East 62nd Street
New York, New York 10021
212/758-6110

Department of Pediatrics
New York Medical College
106th Street and Fifth Avenue
New York, New York 10029
212/860-8000

The Door—A Center of
Alternatives
618 Avenue of the Americas
New York, New York 10011
212/691-6161

Eastern Women's Center
14 East 60th Street
New York, New York 10022
212/832-0033

Greater New York Division
Social Services for Children
50 West 23rd Street
New York, New York 10010
212/255-9400

Jewish Board of Family and
Children's Services
120 West 57th Street
New York, New York 10019
212/582-9100

Maternity Center Association
48 East 92nd Street
New York, New York 10028
212/369-7300

Parkmed
475 Park Avenue South
New York, New York 10016
212/725-9640 or 683-4100

Planned Parenthood of New York
City, Inc.
380 Second Avenue, Third Floor
New York, New York 10010
212/777-2002

*Project Contact
New York, New York
212/533-3570

Thomas Askin Youth Project
307 Brighton Beach Avenue
New York, New York
212/934-8025

Washington Heights Medical
Service Group
276 Fifth Avenue
New York, New York 10022
212/689-3939

Family and Children's Service of
  Niagara
826 Chilton Avenue
Niagara Falls, New York 14301
716/285-6984

Planned Parenthood of Niagara
  County
906 Michigan Avenue
Niagara Falls, New York 14305
716/282-1223

Planned Parenthood Association
  of Delaware & Otsego
  Counties, Inc.
48 Market Street
Oneonta, New York 13820
607/432-2250

Planned Parenthood of Clinton
  County
66 Brinkerhoff Street
Plattsburgh, New York 12901
518/561-4430

Family Services of Dutchess
  County
50 North Hamilton Street
Poughkeepsie, New York 12601
914/425-1110

Planned Parenthood of
  Dutchess-Ulster
85 Market Street
Poughkeepsie, New York 12601
914/471-1540

Family Service of Rochester
30 North Clinton Avenue
Rochester, New York 14604
716/232-1840

Planned Parenthood of Rochester
  and Monroe County, Inc.
24 Windsor Street
Rochester, New York 14605
716/546-2595

Planned Parenthood of
  Schenectady and Affiliated
  Counties, Inc.
414 Union Street
Schenectady, New York 12305
518/374-5353

*Seabury Barn Crisis Line
Stony Brook, New York
516/751-1411

Planned Parenthood Center of
  Syracuse, Inc.
1120 East Genesee Street
Syracuse, New York 13210
315/475-5525

Planned Parenthood Association
  of Mohawk Valley
1424 Genesee Street
Utica, New York 13502
315/724-6146

Planned Parenthood of Northern
  New York, Inc.
161 Stone Street
Watertown, New York 13601
315/782-1818

Planned Parenthood of Rockland
  County
37 Village Square
West Nyack, New York 10994
914/358-1145

Planned Parenthood of
   Westchester, Inc.
88 East Post Road
White Plains, New York 10601
914/428-7876

Westchester Women's Health
   Organization
20 Church Street
White Plains, New York 10601
914/761-9200

NORTH CAROLINA

Family Counseling Service
Allen Center
331 College Street
Asheville, North Carolina 28801
704/253-9314

Planned Parenthood of
   Asheville/Buncombe County,
   Inc.
131 McDowell Street
Asheville, North Carolina 28801
704/252-7928

Family and Children's Service
301 South Brevard Street
Charlotte, North Carolina 28202
704/332-9034

Florence Crittenton Services
P.O. Box 36392
Charlotte, North Carolina 28236
704/372-4663

Planned Parenthood of Greater
   Charlotte
East Independence Plaza Building
951 South Independence
   Boulevard
Charlotte, North Carolina 28202
704/377-0841

*The Relatives Crisis Line
Charlotte, North Carolina
704/377-0602

Family Counseling Service of
   Durham
1200 Broad Street
Durham, North Carolina 27705
919/286-3757

Women's Pavilion
2634 Chapel Hill Boulevard
Durham, North Carolina 27704
919/493-2556

Family and Children's Services
1301 North Elm Street
Greensboro, North Carolina
   27401
919/373-1341

Family Counseling Service of
   Gaston County
318 South Street
Gastonia, North Carolina 28052
704/864-7704

Women's Pavilion
823 North Elm Street
Greensboro, North Carolina
   27403
919/274-3771

Family Guidance Center
#17 Highway 64-70, S.E.
Hickory, North Carolina 28601
704/322-1400

Family Service Bureau
410 Gatewood Avenue
High Point, North Carolina 27260
919/889-6161

Family Services of Wake County
3803 Computer Drive
Raleigh, North Carolina 27609
919/781-9317

The Fleming Center, Inc.
3613 Haworth Drive
Raleigh, North Carolina 27698
919/781-5550

Planned Parenthood of Greater
  Raleigh
1300 St. Mary's Street
Raleigh, North Carolina 27605
919/833-7526

Family Service
208 First Union National Bank
  Building
Wilmington, North Carolina
  28402
919/763-5189

Family Services
610 Coliseum Drive
Winston-Salem, North Carolina
  27106
919/722-8173

Planned Parenthood of Greater
  Winston-Salem, Inc.
129 Fayette Street
Winston-Salem, North Carolina
  27101
919/761-1052

OHIO

Akron Center for Reproductive
  Health
839 East Market Street
Akron, Ohio 44305
216/535-9191

Catholic Service League
640 North Main Street
Akron, Ohio 44310
216/762-7481

Family Services of Summit
  County
212 East Exchange Street
Akron, Ohio 44304
216/376-9494

Jewish Family Service
3085 West Market Street
Akron, Ohio 44313
216/867-3388

Planned Parenthood Association
  of Summit County, Inc.
29 East Market Street
Akron, Ohio 44308
216/535-2671

Teenage Parent Center
220 South Broadway
Akron, Ohio 44308
216/535-3117

Planned Parenthood of Southeast
  Ohio
306 Security Building
Athens, Ohio 45701
614/593-3375

Family Counseling Services
618 Second Street, N.W.
Canton, Ohio 44703
216/454-7066

Planned Parenthood of Stark
  County
626 Walnut Avenue, N.E.
Canton, Ohio 44702
216/456-7191

Adolescent Service
Cincinnati General Hospital
Cincinnati, Ohio 45229
513/559-4681

Catharine Booth Home
3595 Washington Avenue
Cincinnati, Ohio 45229
513/751-6900

Family Service of the Cincinnati
  Area
2343 Auburn Avenue
Cincinnati, Ohio 45219
513/381-6300

Jewish Family Service
1710 Section Road
Cincinnati, Ohio 45237
513/351-3680

*The Lighthouse Crisis Line
Cincinnati, Ohio
513/961-4080

Planned Parenthood Association
  of Cincinnati
2406 Auburn Avenue
Cincinnati, Ohio 45219
513/721-7993

Women for Women of Cincinnati,
  Inc.
411 Oak Street
Cincinnati, Ohio 45219
513/961-7615

Pickaway Family Planning
  Association
Berger Hospital
600 North Pickaway
Circleville, Ohio 43113
614/374-5143

Booth Memorial Home and
  Hospital
1881 Torbenson Drive
Cleveland, Ohio 44112
216/692-3500

Catholic Counseling Center
1001 Huron Road
Cleveland, Ohio 44115
216/696-6650

Cleveland Center for
  Reproductive Health
1195 Shaker Boulevard
Cleveland Ohio 44120
216/421-8600

Cleveland Clinic Foundation
Adolescent Diagnostic Center
9500 Euclid Avenue
Cleveland, Ohio 44106
216/444-5516

Department of Pediatrics
Adolescent Clinic
Cleveland Metropolitan General
  Hospital
3395 Scranton Road
Cleveland, Ohio 44109
216/398-6000

Jewish Family Service
  Association of Cleveland
2060 South Taylor Road
Cleveland, Ohio 44118
216/371-2600

Omni Health Center
5 Severance Circle
Cleveland Heights, Ohio 44118
216/382-6050

Planned Parenthood of
Cleveland, Inc.
2027 Cornell Road
Cleveland, Ohio 44106
216/721-4700

Pre-term Cleveland
10900 Carnegie Avenue
Cleveland, Ohio 44106
216/368-1006

Crittenton Service Center
1229 Sunbury Road
Columbus, Ohio 43219
614/262-5229

Family Counseling and Crittenton
Services
199 South Fifth Street
Columbus, Ohio 43215
614/221-7608

Family Counseling East
3901 East Livingston Avenue
Columbus, Ohio 43227
614/236-8733

Family Counseling North
4770 Indianola Avenue
Columbus, Ohio 43214
614/885-8259

Family Counseling Northwest
1560 Fishinger Road
Columbus, Ohio 43221
614/457-8237

Family Life Center
802-804 East Main Street
Columbus, Ohio 43205
614/252-0901

*Huckleberry House Crisis Line
Columbus, Ohio
614/294-5553

Jewish Family Service
1175 College Avenue
Columbus, Ohio 43209
614/231-1890

Planned Parenthood of Central
Ohio, Inc.
206 East State Street
Columbus, Ohio 43215
614/224-2235

Northeast Summit Family Service
507 Portage Trail
Cuyahoga Falls, Ohio 44221
216/928-1159

*Daybreak Crisis Line
Dayton, Ohio
513/461-1000

Dayton Women's Health Center,
Inc.
3460 South Dixie Drive
Dayton, Ohio 45439
513/296-1306

Family Service Association
184 Salem Avenue
Dayton, Ohio 45406
513/222-9481

Planned Parenthood Association
of Miami Valley
224 North Wilkinson Street
Dayton, Ohio 45402
513/226-0780

Maternal Health Association of
Lorain County
502 Middle Avenue
Elyria, Ohio 44035
216/322-9874

Planned Parenthood Association
of Crawford County
777 Portland Way North
Galion, Ohio 44833
419/468-9926

Family Service of Butler County
111 Buckeye Street
Hamilton, Ohio 45011
513/868-3245

Planned Parenthood Association
of Butler County
P.O. Box 631
11 Ludlow Street
Hamilton, Ohio 45012
513/894-8335

Child and Family Service
616 South Collett Street
Lima, Ohio 45805
419/225-1040

Family Service Association of
Lorain County
4370 Oberlin Avenue
Lorain, Ohio 44053
216/282-4273

Planned Parenthood Association
of the Mansfield Area
35 North Park Street
Mansfield, Ohio 44902
419/525-3075

Family Counseling Services of
Western Stark County
11 Lincoln Way, West
Massillon, Ohio 44646
216/832-5043

Family Service Association of
Licking County
122 West Church Street
Newark, Ohio 43055
614/345-4920

Planned Parenthood Association
of East Central Ohio
Newark Medical Center
843 North 21st Street
Newark, Ohio 43055
614/366-3377

*Together Crisis Line
Oxford, Ohio
513/523-4146

Family Planned Association of
Lake and Geauga Counties
1499 Mentor Avenue
Painsville, Ohio 44077
215/352-0608

Family Service Agency of
Springfield and Clark County
Tecumseh Building
34 West High Street
Springfield, Ohio 45502
513/325-5564

Family Service Association
248 North Fifth Street
Steubenville, Ohio 43952
614/283-4763

Planned Parenthood of West
  Central Ohio
Arcue Building, 5th Floor
6 West High Street
Springfield, Ohio 45502
513/325-6416

Family Services of Greater Toledo
1 Stranahan Square
Toledo, Ohio 43604
419/244-5511

Planned Parenthood of Greater
  Toledo, Inc.
1301 Jefferson
Toledo, Ohio 43624
419/255-1115

Teen Health Clinic
St. Vincent Hospital and Medical
  Center
2213 Cherry Street
Toledo, Ohio 43608
419/259-4795

Toledo Crittenton Services
3151 Chollett Drive
Toledo, Ohio 43606
419/475-8681

Family Service Association
1704 North Road, S.E.
Warren, Ohio 44484
216/856-2907

Planned Parenthood of Wayne
  County
2680½ Cleveland Road
Wooster, Ohio 44691
216/345-7798

*Daybreak Crisis Line
Youngstown, Ohio
216/746-8410

Planned Parenthood of
  Mahoning Valley
105 East Boardman Street
Youngstown, Ohio 44503
216/746-5662

Family Service Agency
535 Marmion
Youngstown, Ohio 44502
216/782-5664

OKLAHOMA

Outpatient Services for Women
4334 N.W. Expressway
Oklahoma City, Oklahoma 73116
405/848-7501

Planned Parenthood Association
  of Oklahoma City
10 N.E. 23rd Street
Oklahoma City, Oklahoma 73105
405/528-2157

Sunbeam Family Services
616 N.W. 21st Street
Oklahoma City, Oklahoma 73103
405/528-7721

Family and Children's Service
650 South Peoria
Tulsa, Oklahoma 74120
918/587-9471

Planned Parenthood of Eastern
 Oklahoma and Western
 Arkansas
1007 South Peoria
Tulsa, Oklahoma 74120
918/587-1101

The Salvation Army Maternity
 Home
7820 West 7th Street
Tulsa, Oklahoma 74127
918/245-1827

OREGON

*Sunflower House Crisis Line
Corvallis, Oregon
503/753-1241

*Looking Glass Crisis Line
Eugene, Oregon
503/689-3111

Planned Parenthood Association
 of Lane County
134 East 13th Avenue
Eugene, Oregon 97401
503/344-9411 or 503/344-1611

Planned Parenthood of Jackson
 County
650 Royal Avenue; Suite 18
Medford, Oregon 97501
503/773-8285

Metropolitan Family Service
2281 N.W. Everett Street
Portland, Oregon 97210
503/228-7238

Planned Parenthood Association,
 Inc.
1200 S.E. Morrison
Portland, Oregon 97214
503/234-5411

Portland Women's Health Center
6510 S.E. Foster Road
Portland, Oregon 97206
503/777-7044

White Shield Home
2640 N.W. Alexandria Avenue
Portland, Oregon 97210
503/226-4054

PENNSYLVANIA

*COMAC Youth Service Crisis
 Line
Abington, Pennsylvania
215/885-6655

Family and Children's Service of
 Lehigh County
411 Walnut Street
Allentown, Pennsylvania 18102
215/435-9651

Planned Parenthood Association
 of Lehigh County
112 N. 13th Street
Allentown, Pennsylvania 18102
215/439-1033

Family Service of Beaver County
1445 Market Street (W.B.)
Beaver, Pennsylvania 15009
412/775-8390

Family Counseling Service of
Northampton County
520 East Broad Street
Bethlehem, Pennsylvania 18018
215/867-3946

*Valley Youth House Crisis Line
Bethlehem, Pennsylvania
215/691-1200

Planned Parenthood Association
of Bucks County
721 New Rodgers Road
Bristol, Pennsylvania 19007
215/785-4591

Reproductive Health and
Counseling Center
Crozer Chester Medical Center
Annex
15th & Upland Avenues
Chester, Pennsylvania 19013
215/874-4361

Family Service Association of
Bucks County
20 West Oakland Avenue
Doylestown, Pennsylvania 18901
215/345-0550

Planned Parenthood of
Northampton County, Inc.
275 South 21st Street
Easton, Pennsylvania 18042
215-253-7195

Monroe County Planned
Parenthood Association
162 East Brown Street
East Stroudsburg, Pennsylvania
18301
717/424-8306

Family Service Association
Sumner East Nichols Building
155 West 8th Street
Erie, Pennsylvania 16501
814/454-6478

Family and Children's Service
121 Locust Street
Harrisburg, Pennsylvania 17101
717/238-8118

Harrisburg Reproductive Health
Services, Inc.
100 Chestnut Street
Harrisburg, Pennsylvania 17101
717/232-9794

Planned Parenthood
Cambria/Somerset
502 Main Street
Johnstown, Pennsylvania 15901
814/535-5545

Women's Medical Center
DeKalb & Boro Line Road
King of Prussia, Pennsylvania
19406
215/265-1880

Family and Children's Service of
Lancaster County
630 Janet Avenue
Lancaster, Pennsylvania 17601
717/397-5241

Planned Parenthood of Lancaster
37 South Lime Street
Lancaster, Pennsylvania 17602
717/299-2891

Family and Community Service
of Delaware County
100 West Front Street
Media, Pennsylvania 19063
215/566-7540

Family Service of Montgomery
County
1906 Swede Road
Norristown, Pennsylvania 19401
215/272-1520

Family Service and Children's Aid
Society of Venango County
202 West First Street
Oil City, Pennsylvania 16301
814/677-4005

Women's Suburban Clinic
1440 Russell Road
Paoli, Pennsylvania 19301
215/647-1344

Booth Maternity Center
6051 Overbrook Avenue
Philadelphia, Pennsylvania 19131
215/878-7800

Center for Human Services of
Episcopal Community Services
225 South Third Street
Philadelphia, Pennsylvania 19106
215/351-1400

Children's Hospital of
Philadelphia
Adolescent Clinic
34th and Civic Center Boulevard
Philadelphia, Pennsylvania 19102
215/387-6311

Elizabeth Blackwell Health Center
for Women
112 South 16th Street
Philadelphia, Pennsylvania 19102
215/563-7577

Family Service of Philadelphia
311 Juniper Street
Philadelphia, Pennsylvania 19107
215/875-3300

Jewish Family Service of
Philadelphia
1610 Spruce Street
Philadelphia, Pennsylvania 19103
215/545-3290

Planned Parenthood Association
of Southeastern Pennsylvania
1220 Sansom Street
Philadelphia, Pennsylvania 19107
215/629-2800

*Voyage House Crisis Line
Philadelphia, Pennsylvania
215/735-8406

*Amicus Crisis Center
Pittsburgh, Pennsylvania
412/621-3653

Booth Memorial Home
2214 Pauline Avenue
Pittsburgh, Pennsylvania 15216
412/561-1242

Family & Children's Service
Clark Building, 18th Floor
717 Liberty Avenue
Pittsburgh, Pennsylvania
15222
412/261-3623

Jewish Family and Children's
Service
234 McKee Place
Pittsburgh, Pennsylvania 15213
412/683-4900

Planned Parenthood Center of
Pittsburgh
102 Ninth Street
Pittsburgh, Pennsylvania 15222
412/434-8950

Planned Parenthood Center of
Berks County
48 South Fourth Street
Reading, Pennsylvania 19602
215/376-8061

Family Service of Lackawanna
County
615 Jefferson Avenue
Scranton, Pennsylvania 18510
717/342-3149

Planned Parenthood of
Lackawanna & Wyoming
Counties
207 Wyoming Avenue; Suite 322
Scranton, Pennsylvania 18503
717/344-2626

Family Services of Warren
County
8 Pennsylvania Avenue, West
Warren, Pennsylvania 16365
814/723-1330

Family Service of Chester County
310 North Matlack Street
West Chester, Pennsylvania 19380
215/696-4900

Planned Parenthood of Chester
County
202 North Church Street
West Chester, Pennsylvania 19380
215/436-8645

Family Service Association of
Wyoming Valley
73 West Union Street
Wilkes-Barre, Pennsylvania 18701
717/823-5144

Planned Parenthood Association
of Luzerne County
63 North Franklin Street
Wilkes-Barre, Pennsylvania 18701
717/824-8921

Family Service of York and York
County
800 East King Street
York, Pennsylvania 17403
717/845-6624

Planned Parenthood of Central
Pennsylvania
728 South Beaver Street
York, Pennsylvania 17403
717/845-9681

RHODE ISLAND

Child and Family Services of
Newport County
24 School Street
Newport, Rhode Island 02840
401/849-2300

Family Service Society of
Pawtucket and Vicinity
33 Summer Street
Pawtucket, Rhode Island 02860
401/723-2124

Family Service
75 Charlesfield Street
Providence, Rhode Island 02906
401/331-1350

Jewish Family Service
229 Waterman Street
Providence, Rhode Island 02906
401/331-1244

Planned Parenthood of Rhode
  Island
187 Westminster Mall
Providence, Rhode Island 02903
401/421-9620

*Sympatico Crisis Line
Wakefield, Rhode Island
401/783-0772

SOUTH CAROLINA

Charleston County Department
  of Social Services
409 County Center
Charleston, South Carolina 2940:
803/729-7290

Family Service of Charleston
  County
Community Services Building
30 Lockwood Boulevard
Charleston, South Carolina 29401
803/723-4566

Family Service Center
1800 Main Street
Columbia, South Carolina 29201
803/779-3250

Planned Parenthood of Central
  South Carolina, Inc.
3101 Carlisle at Butler Street
Columbia, South Carolina 29205
803/256-4908

Southern Women's Services
1614 Two Notch Road
Columbia, South Carolina 29204
803/254-4368

Family Counseling Service
108 Three Hundred Building
300 University Ridge
Greenville, South Carolina 29603
803/232-2434

Greenville Hospital Systems
Adolescent Clinic
Department of Pediatric
  Education
Greenville General Hospital
Greenville, South Carolina 29601
803/242-7000

Service to Families
830 North Church Street
Spartanburg, South Carolina
  29303
803/573-6762

SOUTH DAKOTA

Family Service
1728 South Cliff Avenue
Sioux Falls, South Dakota 57105
605/336-1974

TENNESSEE

Family and Children's Services of
  Chattanooga
323 High Street
Chattanooga, Tennessee 37403
615/267-0021

Child and Family Services of
  Knox County
114 Dameron Avenue
Knoxville, Tennessee 37917
615/524-7483

The Florence Crittenton Agency
P.O. Box 4094
Knoxville, Tennessee 37921
615/522-9601

Knoxville Center for
  Reproductive Health
1547 West Clinch Avenue
Knoxville, Tennessee 37916
615/637-3861

Family Service of Memphis
2400 Poplar Building,
Suite 500
Memphis, Tennessee 38112
901/324-3637

Memphis Association for Planned
  Parenthood, Inc.
1407 Union Avenue
Memphis, Tennessee 38104
901/725-1717

Family and Children's Service
201 23rd Avenue, North
Nashville, Tennessee 37203
615/327-0833

Florence Crittenton Home and
  Services
1815 Division Street
Nashville, Tennessee 37203
615/327-0340

Planned Parenthood Association
  of Nashville
University Plaza
112 21st Avenue South
Nashville, Tennessee 37203
615/327-1066 or 615/327-1095

Planned Parenthood of East
  Tennessee, Inc.
162 Ridgeway Center
Oak Ridge, Tennessee 37830
615/482-3406

TEXAS

Amarillo Guidance and
  Counseling Center
900 South Lincoln
Amarillo, Texas 79101
806/372-3202

Panhandle Planned Parenthood
  Association
604 West Eighth Street
Amarillo, Texas 79101
806/372-8731

Child and Family Service
419 West Sixth Street
Austin, Texas 78701
512/478-1648

Planned Parenthood of Austin
1823 East 7th Street
Austin, Texas 78702
512/477-7050

Family Services Association
447 Orleans Street, Suite 211
Beaumont, Texas 77701
713/833-2668

Planned Parenthood of Cameron
  and Willacy Counties
15 East Levee Street
Brownsville, Texas 78520
512/546-4571

Family Counseling Service
507 South Water Street
Corpus Christi, Texas 78401
512/882-2546

South Texas Planned Parenthood
  Center
801 Elizabeth Street
Corpus Christi, Texas 78404
512/884-4352

Family Guidance Center
2200 Main Street
Dallas, Texas 75201
214/747-8331

Planned Parenthood of Greater
  Dallas, Inc.
5728 LBJ Freeway, Suite 400
Dallas, Texas 75240
214/239-3831

University of Texas
Southwestern Medical School
Department of Pediatrics
Dallas, Texas 75207
214/688-2925

Family Service of El Paso
2930 North Stanton Street
El Paso, Texas 79902
915/533-2491

Planned Parenthood Center of El
  Paso
214 West Franklin Street
El Paso, Texas 79901
915/542-1919

Family and Individual Services
  Association of Tarrant County
716 West Magnolia
Fort Worth, Texas 76104
817/335-2401

Planned Parenthood of North
  Texas
327 South Adams
Fort Worth, Texas 76104
817/332-7966

Pregnancy Control, Inc.
1201 West Presidio
Fort Worth, Texas 76102
817/335-6641

Adolescent Division
University of Texas Medical
  Branch
Galveston, Texas 77550
713/765-2355

Family Service Center of
  Galveston County
926 Broadway
Galveston, Texas 77550
713/762-8636

*Galveston YWCA Crisis Line
Galveston, Texas
713/763-8861

Family Service Center
5049 39th Street, Suite C
Groves, Texas 77619
713/963-0159

*The Family Connection Crisis
  Line
Houston, Texas
713/523-6825

Family Service Center
3635 West Dallas
Houston, Texas 7701
713/524-3881

Florence Crittenton Services
5107 Scotland Street
Houston, Texas 77007
713/869-7221

Jewish Family Service
4131 South Braeswood Boulevard
Houston, Texas 77025
713/667-9336

Planned Parenthood of Houston
  and Southeast Texas
3601 Fannin
Houston, Texas 77004
713/522-3976

Reproductive Services, Inc.
6441 High Star
Houston, Texas 77074
713/771-4336

Women's Pavilion
330 Meadowfern, #107
Houston, Texas 77067
713/893-7080

Planned Parenthood Association
  of Chaparral County
529 East King, P.O. Box 1070
Kingsville, Texas 78363
512/592-2201

Planned Parenthood Center of
  Lubbock
3821 22nd Street
Lubbock, Texas 79413
806/795-7123

Planned Parenthood Association
  of Hidalgo County
1017 Pecan
McAllen, Texas 78501
512/686-0585

Family Services of Midland
9 Rivercrest Building
2101 West Wall
Midland, Texas 79701
915/683-4241

Permian Basin Planned
  Parenthood, Inc.
910-B South Grant Street
Odessa, Texas 79763
915/563-2530

Planned Parenthood Center of
  San Angelo
122 West Second Street
San Angelo, Texas 76901
915/655-9141

Adolescent Medicine Service
Department of Pediatrics
Brooke Army Medical Center
San Antonio, Texas 78234
512/221-4407 or 512/221-6735

Family Service Association of San
  Antonio
230 Pereida Street
San Antonio, Texas 78210
512/226-3391

Jewish Family Service
8438 Ahern Drive
San Antonio, Texas 78218
512/349-5481

Planned Parenthood Center of
   San Antonio
106 Warren Street
San Antonio, Texas 78212
512/227-2227

The Central Texas Planned
   Parenthood Association
P.O. Box 6308
1121 Ross Avenue
Waco, Texas 76706
817/754-2392

Family Counseling and Children's
   Services
213 Community Services Building
201 West Waco Drive, P.O. Box
   464
Waco, Texas 76703
817/753-1509

Reproductive Services
Suite 206 Fre-Mar Valley
3100 Seymour Highway
Wichita, Texas 76301
817/322-9637

UTAH

Planned Parenthood Association
   of Utah
70 South 900 East #13
Salt Lake City, Utah 84103
801/322-5571

Utah Women's Clinic
515 S. 400 East
Salt Lake City, Utah 84111
801/531-9192

VERMONT

Planned Parenthood of Vermont
23 Mansfield Avenue
Burlington, Vermont 05401
802/862-9637

*Spectrum Crisis Line
Burlington, Vermont
802/864-7423

Vermont Women's Health Center,
   Inc.
336 North Avenue
Burlington, Vermont 05401
802/863-1386

VIRGINIA

Charlottesville Obstetrical
   Associates, Inc.
1933 Arlington Boulevard
Charlottesville, Virginia 22903
804/977-0200

Social Service Bureau
Municipal Building, P.O. Box
   3300
Danville, Virginia 24541
804/799-6537

Northern Virginia Women's
   Medical Center
3918 Prosperity Avenue
Fairfax, Virginia 22031
703/280-1500

Planned Parenthood of Northern
   Virginia
5622 Columbia Pike
Falls Church, Virginia 22041
703/820-3335

Northern Virginia Family Service
100 North Washington Street
Falls Church, Virginia 22046
703/533-9727

Peninsula Family Service
1520 Aberdeen Road
P.O. Box 7315
Hampton, Virginia 23666
804/838-1960

Planned Parenthood of
   Southeastern Virginia
1520 Aberdeen Road, Room 101
Hampton, Virginia 23666
804/826-2079

Family Service of Central Virginia
1010 Miller Park Square
Lynchburg, Virginia 24501
804/845-5944

*Alternative House Crisis Line
McLean, Virginia
703/356-6360

Adolescent Medicine
Department of Pediatrics
Children's Hospital of the King's
   Daughters
609 Colley Avenue
Norfolk, Virginia 23507
804/622-1381

Family Service
222 19th Street
Norfolk, Virginia 23517
804/622-7017

Planned Parenthood of Tidewater
712 Botetourt Street
Norfolk, Virginia 23507
804/625-5591

Adolescent Clinic
Department of Pediatrics
Naval Region Medical Center
Portsmouth, Virginia 23708
804/397-6541

Child and Family Service
355 Crawford Street
Portsmouth, Virginia 23704
804/397-2121 or 804/397-3311

Family and Children's Service of
   Richmond
1518 Willow Lawn Drive
Richmond, Virginia 23230
804/282-4255

Jewish Family Services
7027 Three Chopt Road
Richmond, Virginia 23226
804/282-5644

MCV Adolescent Clinic
Medical College of Virginia
Box 151
Richmond, Virginia 23298
804/770-6506

*Oasis House Crisis Line
Richmond, Virginia
804/329-0079

Virginia League for Planned
   Parenthood, Inc.
1218 West Franklin Street
Richmond, Virginia 23220
804/353-5516

Family Service of Roanoke Valley
518 Carlton Terrace Building
920 South Jefferson Street
Roanoke, Virginia 24016
703/344-3253

Planned Parenthood of Roanoke
  Valley, Inc.
309 Luck Avenue, S.W.
Roanoke, Virginia 24016
703/342-6741

*Roanoke Valley Trouble Center
  Crisis Line
Roanoke, Virginia
703/563-0311

Tri-County Area Planned
  Parenthood
P.O. Box 1400
Suffolk, Virginia 23434
804/539-3456

WASHINGTON

Proctor Medical Center
1200 112th, N.E.
Bellevue, Washington 98004
206/454-6934

Mt. Baker Planned Parenthood
500 Grand Avenue
Bellingham, Washington 98225
206/734-9095

Planned Parenthood of
  Snohomish County
2730 Hoyt Avenue
Everett, Washington 98201
206/259-0096

Planned Parenthood of Benton-
  Franklin Counties
P.O. Box 6842
Kennewick, Washington 99336
509/586-2164

Family Services of King County
500 Lowman Building
107 Cherry Street
Seattle, Washington 98104
206/447-3883

Group Health Cooperative
10200 First, Northeast
Seattle, Washington 98125
206/447-2350

Planned Parenthood of Seattle-
  King County
2211 East Madison
Seattle, Washington 98112
206/447-2350 or 206/447-2364

Family Counseling Service
369 Paulsen Building
Spokane, Washington 99201
509/838-4128

Planned Parenthood of Spokane
West 521 Garland Avenue
Spokane, Washington 99205
509/326-6292 or 509/326-2142

Family Counseling Service
1008 South Yakima Avenue
Tacoma, Washington 98405
206/627-6105

Planned Parenthood of Pierce
  County
312 Broadway Terrace Building
Tacoma, Washington 98402
206/572-6955

Planned Parenthood of Walla
  Walla
136 East Birch Street
Walla Walla, Washington 99362
509/529-3570

Planned Parenthood Association
of Yakima County
208 North Third Avenue
Yakima, Washington 98902
509/248-3625

WEST VIRGINIA

Women's Health Center of West
Virginia, Inc.
3418 Staunton Avenue, S.E.
Charleston, West Virginia 25304
304/344-9838

Family Service of Marion and
Harrison Counties
201 Virginia Ave.
P.O. Box 1265
Fairmont, West Virginia 26554
304/366-4750

Planned Parenthood Association
of Parkersburg
1100 Market St.
P.O. Box 1095
Parkersburg, West Virginia 26101
304/485-1144

Children and Family Service
Association
109 North Main Street
Wheeling, West Virginia 26003
304/233-6300

WISCONSIN

Fox Valley Planned Parenthood
508 West Wisconsin Avenue
Appleton, Wisconsin 54911
414/731-6304

Lakeland Area Planned
Parenthood
138 Front Street
Beaver Dam, Wisconsin 53916
414/885-3528

Family Service Association of
Beloit
423 Bluff Street
Beloit, Washington 53511
608/365-1244

Bay-Lakes Planned Parenthood
302 North Adams Street
Green Bay, Wisconsin 54301
414/432-0031

Beaumont Clinic, Ltd.
Pediatric and Adolescent
Department
1821 South Webster Avenue
Green Bay, Wisconsin 54301
414/437-9051

Family Service Association of
Brown County
1546 Dousman Street
Green Bay, Wisconsin 54303
414/499-8768

Kenosha-Walworth Planned
Parenthood
2002 63rd Street
Kenosha, Wisconsin 54220
414/645-0491

Family Service Association
2350 South Avenue
LaCrosse, Wisconsin 54601
608/788-6762

Dane-Sauk-Columbia Planned
  Parenthood
1050 Regent Street
Madison, Wisconsin 53715
608/256-7257

Family Service
214 North Hamilton Street
Madison, Wisconsin 53703
608/251-7611

Madison Gynecology Clinic
1 South Park Street
Madison, Wisconsin 53715
608/251-5900

Teenage Clinic
University of Wisconsin Hospitals
1552 University Avenue
Madison, Wisconsin 53705
608/262-1170

Marshfield Clinic
Adolescent Section and Clinic
1000 North Oak
Marshfield, Wisconsin 54449
715/387-5413 or 715/387-5251

Family Service Association of the
  Fox Valley
929 Midway Road
1488 Kenwood Center
Menasha, Wisconsin 54952
414/739-4226

Bread and Roses Women's Health
  Center, Inc.
238 West Wisconsin Avenue
Milwaukee, Wisconsin 53203
414/278-0260

Family Service of Milwaukee
2819 West Highland Boulevard
Milwaukee, Wisconsin 53208
414/342-4558

Jewish Family and Children's
  Service
1360 North Prospect Avenue
Milwaukee, Wisconsin 53202
414/273-6515

Milwaukee Children's Hospital
  and Adolescent Clinic
1700 West Wisconsin Avenue
Milwaukee, Wisconsin 53202
414/344-7100

*Pathfinders Crisis Line
Milwaukee, Wisconsin
414/271-1560

Planned Parenthood Association
  of Wisconsin, Inc.
1135 West State Street
Milwaukee, Wisconsin 53233
414/271-8116

Summit Medical Center
606 West Wisconsin
Milwaukee, Wisconsin 53203
414/289-9900

Family Service of Racine
420 Seventh Street
Racine, Wisconsin 53403
414/634-2391

*Hot Line
Racine, Wisconsin
414/637-9557

Family Service of Waukesha
County
414 West Moreland Boulevard
Waukesha, Wisconsin 53186
414/547-5567

Kettle Moraine Planned
Parenthood
St. Joseph's Community Hospital
551 Silverbrook Drive
West Bend, Wisconsin 53095
414/338-1303

Central Wisconsin Planned
Parenthood
130 2nd St. North, P.O. Box 941
Wisconsin Rapids, Wisconsin
54494
715/423-9610

WYOMING

For Information call:
Planned Parenthood Western
Region Office
150 Green Street, Suite 3A
San Francisco, California 94111
415/956-8856
or:
Rocky Mountain Planned
Parenthood
1537 Alton Street
Aurora, Colorado 80010
303/360-0006

YWCA Teen Pregnancy Program List

EASTERN SEABOARD

YWCA of Darien, Inc.
49 Old Kingshighway, No.
Darien, Connecticut 06820
203/655-2535

YWCA of Greater Bridgeport,
Inc.
1962 East Main Street
Bridgeport, Connecticut 06610
203/334-6154

YWCA of Meriden
169 Colony Street
Meriden, Connecticut 06450
203/235-9297

YWCA of New Britain
22 Glen Street
New Britain, Connecticut 06051
203/225-4681

YWCA of New Haven
48 Howe Street
New Haven, Connecticut 06511
203/865-5171

YWCA of New London
476 Thames Street
Groton, Connecticut 06340
203/455-8151

YWCA of of Waterbury
80 Prospect Street
Waterbury, Connecticut 06702
203/754-5136

YWCA of of Daytona Beach
344 S. Beach Street
Daytona Beach, Florida 32014
904/252-4769

YWCA of Pensacola
1417 N. 12th Avenue
Pensacola, Florida 32503
904/432-5495

YWCA of St. Petersburg
647 First Avenue, No.
St. Petersburg, Florida 33701
813/896-4629

YWCA of Augusta
924 Greene Street
Augusta, Georgia 30902
404/738-6678

YWCA of Brunswick
1311 Union Street
Brunswick, Georgia 31520
912/265-4100

YWCA of Lewiston-Auburn
248 Turner Street
Auburn, Maine 04210
207/782-1752

YWCA of the Greater Baltimore
  Area
128 West Franklin Street
Baltimore, Maryland 21201
301/685-1460

YWCA of Lowell
29 Hanks Street
Lowell, Massachusetts 01852
617/454-5405

YWCA of Manchester
72 Concord Street
Manchester, New Hampshire
03101
603/625-5785

YWCA of Essex and West
  Hudson
395 Main Street
Orange, New Jersey 07050
201/672-9500

YWCA of Jersey City
270 Fairmont Avenue
Jersey City, New Jersey 07306
201/333-5700

YWCA of Lakewood and Ocean
  County
Monmouth Ave./3rd Street
Lakewood, New Jersey 08701
201/363-1158

YWCA of Montclair-North Essex
159 Glenridge Avenue
Montclair, New Jersey 07042
201/746-5400

YWCA of Princeton
Paul Robeson Place
Princeton, New Jersey 08540
609/924-5571

YWCA of Binghamton and
  Broome County
Hawley and Exchange Streets
Binghamton, New York 13901
607/772-0340

YWCA of Buffalo and Erie
   County
190 Franklin Street
Buffalo, New York 14202
716/852-6120

YWCA of Dutchess County
18 Bancroft Road
Poughkeepsie, New York 12601
914/454-6770

YWCA of Elmira
211 Lake Street
Elmira, New York 14901
607/733-5575

YWCA of Jamestown
401 N. Main Street
Jamestown, New York 14701
716/485-1137

YWCA of Ulster County
209 Clinton Avenue
Kingston, New York 14701
914/338-6844

YWCA of Lockport
32 Cottage Street
Lockport, New York 14094
716/433-6714

YWCA of Niagara Falls
567 Main Street
Niagara Falls, New York 14301
716/282-1273

YWCA of Peekskill
1028 Main Street
Peekskill, New York 10566
914/737-2095

YWCA of Rochester and Monroe
   County
175 Clinton Avenue, No.
Rochester, New York 14604
716/546-5820

YWCA of Schenectady
44 Washington Avenue
Schenectady, New York 12305
518/373-3394

YWCA of Syracuse and
   Onondaga County
339 East Onondaga Street
Syracuse, New York 13202
315/445-2200

YWCA of Troy and Cohoes, New
   York, Inc.
21 First Street
Troy, New York 12180
518/274-7100

YWCA of Asheville
185 S. French Broad Ave.
Asheville, North Carolina
28801
704/254-7206

YWCA of Durham
809 Proctor Street
Durham, North Carolina 27707
919/688-4396

YWCA of Greensboro
314 N. Davie Street
Greensboro, North Carolina
27401
919/273-3461

YWCA of Raleigh, Inc.
1012 Oberlin Road
Raleigh, North Carolina 27605
919/828-3205

YWCA of Winston-Salem and
  Forsyth County
1201 Glade Street
Winston-Salem, North
Carolina 27101
919/722-5138

YWCA of Bradford
24 West Corydon Street
Bradford, Pennsylvania 16701
814/368-4235

YWCA of Bucks County
102 W. Maple Street
P.O. Box 335
Langhorne, Pennsylvania 19047
215/757-3782

YWCA of Germantown
5820 Germantown Avenue
Philadelphia, Pennsylvania
19144
215/438-6266

YWCA of Gettysburg
8 Lincoln Square
Gettysburg, Pennsylvania 17325
717/334-6112

YWCA of Greater Pittsburgh
Fourth/Wood Streets
Pittsburgh, Pennsylvania 15222
412/391-5100

YWCA of Greater West Chester
123 N. Church Street
West Chester, Pennsylvania
19380
215/692-3737

YWCA of Greensburg
424 No. Main Street
Greensburg, Pennsylvania
15601
412/834-9390

YWCA of Hazelton
75 So. Church Street
Hazelton, Pennsylvania 18201
717/455-2046

YWCA of Lancaster
110 N. Lime Street
Lancaster, Pennsylvania 17331
717/393-1735

YWCA of Oil City
109 Central Avenue
Oil City, Pennsylvania 16301
814/676-6528

YWCA of Reading
8th and Washington Streets
Reading, Pennsylvania 19601
215/376-7317

YWCA of Titusville
201 N. Franklin Street
Titusville, Pennsylvania 16354
814/827-2746

YWCA of Washington
42 West Maiden Street
Washington, Pennsylvania
17872
412/222-3200

YWCA of York
320 East Market Street
York, Pennsylvania 17403
717/845-2631

YWCA of Richmond
6 North Fifth Street
Richmond, Virginia 23219
804/643-6761

YWCA of Roanoke Valley
605 First Street, S.W.
Roanoke, Virginia 24011
703/344-6234

YWCA of the Tidewater Areas
253 Freemason Street
Norfolk, Virginia 23510
804/625-4248

YWCA of Buckhannon
167 Camden Avenue
Buckhannon, West Virginia
26201
304/472-9374

MIDWEST

YWCA of Greater Little Rock
112 East Fourth Street
Little Rock, Arkansas 72201
501/664-4268

YWCA of Hot Springs
500 Quapaw Avenue
Hot Springs, Arkansas 71901
501/623-1686

YWCA of Freeport
641 W. Stephenson
Freeport, Illinois 61032
815/235-9421

YWCA of Metropolitan
  Chicago
37 S. Wabash Avenue
Chicago, Illinois 60603
312/372-6600

YWCA of Rockford
220 South Madison Street
Rockford, Illinois 61101
815/968-9681

YWCA of Lake County
412 North Genesee Street
Waukegan, Illinois 60085
312/662-4242

YWCA of Rock Island
229 16th Street
Rock Island, Illinois 61201
309/788-3479

YWCA of Anderson
304 West 11th Street
Anderson, Indiana 46016
317/642-0211

YWCA of Elkhart County
200 East Jackson Boulevard
Elkhart, Indiana 46514
219/295-6915

YWCA of Evansville
118 Vine Street
Evansville, Indiana 47708
812/422-1191

YWCA of Fort Wayne
2000 North Wells Street
Fort Wayne, Indiana 46808
219/424-4908

YWCA of Gary
30 East 6th Avenue
Gary, Indiana 46402
219/886-9196

YWCA of Kokomo
406 E. Sycamore
Kokomo, Indiana 46901
317/457-3293

YWCA of Lafayette
605 N. 6th Street
Lafayette, Indiana 47901
317/742-0075

YWCA of Muncie
310 East Charles Street
Muncie, Indiana 47305
317/284-3345

YWCA of Terre Haute
951 Dresser Drive
Terre Haute, Indiana 47807
812/232-3358

YWCA of Burlington
409 N. 4th Street
Burlington, Iowa 52601
319/753-6734

YWCA of Cedar Rapids and
  Linn County
318 Fifth Street, S.E.
Cedar Rapids, Iowa 52401
319/365-1458

YWCA of Muscatine
309 Sycamore Street
Muscatine, Iowa 52761
319/263-7924

YWCA of Waterloo and Black
  Hawk Co.
425 Lafayette
Waterloo, Iowa 50703
319/234-7589

YWCA of Kansas District
137 North Hillside
Wichita, Kansas 67214
316/682-9261

YWCA of Wichita
350 North Market
Wichita, Kansas 67202
316/263-7501

YWCA of Lexington
1060 Cross Keys Road
Lexington, Kentucky 40504
606/276-4457

YWCA of Shreveport
710 Travis Street
Shreveport, Louisiana 71101
318/222-2116

YWCA of Grand Rapids
25 Sheldon Boulevard, S.E.
Grand Rapids, Michigan 49503
616/459-4681

YWCA of Greater Lansing
217 Townsend
Lansing, Michigan 48733
517/485-7201

YWCA of Metropolitan Detroit
2230 Witherell Street
Detroit, Michigan 48201
313/961-9220

YWCA of Mankato
603 South Second Street
Mankato, Minnesota 56001
507/345-4629

YWCA of Minneapolis Area
1130 Nicollet Avenue
Minneapolis, Minnesota 55403
612/332-0501

YWCA of St. Paul
65 E. Kellogg Boulevard
St. Paul, Minnesota 55101
612/222-3741

YWCA of Winona
223 Center Street
Winona, Minnesota 55987
507/454-4345

YWCA of Jackson
226 North State Street
Jackson, Mississippi 39201
601/352-3036

YWCA of Mississippi District
P.O. Box 942-325 Duncan
  Avenue
Jackson, Mississippi 39205
601/355-6441

YWCA of Kansas City
1000 Charlotte
Kansas City, Missouri 64106
816/842-7538

YWCA of Metropolitan St.
  Louis
1015 Locust Street
St. Louis, Missouri 63101
314/421-2750

YWCA of Beatrice
405 North 5th Street
Beatrice, Nebraska 68310
402/223-5314

YWCA of Minot
205 Third Avenue, S.E.
Minot, North Dakota 58701
701/838-1726

YWCA of Canton
231 Sixth Street, N.E.
Canton, Ohio 44702
216/453-7644

YWCA of Cleveland
3201 Euclid Avenue
Cleveland, Ohio 44115
216/881-6878

YWCA of Dayton
141 West Third Street
Dayton, Ohio 45402
513/461-5550

YWCA of Elyria
318 West Avenue
Elyria, Ohio 44035
216/322-6308

YWCA of Toledo
1018 Jefferson Avenue
Toledo, Ohio 43624
419/241-3235

YWCA of Warren
375 North Park Avenue, N.E.
Warren, Ohio 44481
216/373-1010

YWCA of Mitchell
201 West Third Avenue
Mitchell, South Dakota 57301
605/996-4311

YWCA of Houston
3515 Allen Parkway
Houston, Texas 77019
713/868-9922

YWCA of Metropolitan Dallas
4621 Ross Avenue
Dallas, Texas 75204
214/827-6850

YWCA of Wausau
613-5th Street
Wausau, Wisconsin 54401
715/842-3381

WESTERN REGION

YWCA of Tucson
302 E. University Boulevard
Tucson, Arizona 85705
602/884-7810

YWCA of Bakersfield
1130 17th Street
Bakersfield, California 93301
805/323-6072

YWCA of the Foothills
131 E. Foothill Boulevard
Glendora, California 91740
213/335-7513

YWCA of Glendale
735 E. Lexington Drive
Glendale, California 91740
213/242-4155

YWCA of Greater Pomona
   Valley
1787 North Garey Avenue
Pomona, California 91767
714/622-1269

YWCA of Los Angeles
1052 West Sixth Street, Suite 315
Los Angeles, California 90017
213/482-3470

YWCA of North Orange
   County
321 North Pomona Avenue
Fullerton, California 92632
714/871-4488

YWCA of Pasadena-Foothill
   Valley
78 North Marengo Avenue
Pasadena, California 91101
213/793-5171

YWCA of Riverside
8172 Magnolia Avenue
Riverside, California 92504
714/688-5531

YWCA of San Francisco
620 Sutter Street
San Francisco, California
94102
415/775-6500

YWCA of Tacoma and Pierce
   County
405 Broadway
Tacoma, Washington 98402
206/272-4181

YWCA of South Orange
  County
1411 North Broadway
Santa Ana, California 92706
714/542-3577

YWCA of Oahu
1040 Richards Street
P.O. Box 337
Honolulu, Hawaii 96813
808/538-7061

YWCA of Pocatello
454 North Garfield
Pocatello, Idaho 83201
208/232-0742

YWCA of Billings
909 Wyoming Avenue
Billings, Montana 59101
406/252-6303

YWCA of Great Falls
220 2nd Street North
Great Falls, Montana 59401
406/452-1315

YWCA of Missoula
1130 West Broadway
Missoula, Montana 59801
406/543-6691

YWCA of Reno-Sparks
1301 Valley Road
Reno, Nevada 89512
702/322-4531

YWCA of Salem
768 State Street
Salem, Oregon 97301
503/581-9922

YWCA of Seattle-King County
1118 Fifth Avenue
Seattle, Washington 98101
206/447-4851

YWCA of Spokane
W. 829 Broadway
Spokane, Washington 99201
509/326-1190

YWCA of Cheyenne
222 East 17th Street
Cheyenne, Wyoming 82001
307/635-5212

Canada

ALBERTA

Calgary Birth Control
  Association
#103 223-12th Avenue, S.W.
Calgary, Alberta T2R 0G9
403/261-9821

Family Planning Clinic
337 Seventh Avenue, S.E.
Calgary, Alberta T2P 2M5
403/264-3454

Planned Parenthood Alberta
#206 223-12th Avenue, S.W.
Calgary, Alberta T2R 0G9
403/265-3360

Catholic Social Services
9518-102 A Avenue
Edmonton, Alberta T5H 0G1
403/424-0651

Family Service Association of
Edmonton
Family Service Building
9919 106th Street
Edmonton, Alberta T5K 1E2
403/423-2831

Planned Parenthood Association
of Edmonton
308 McLeod Building
10136-100 Street
Edmonton, Alberta T5J 0P1
403/421-3419 or 423-3737

South Peace Planned Parenthood
10801-100 Street
Grande Prairie, Alberta T8V 2M7
403/532-4461

Center for Personal and
Community Development
205 Professional Building
740-4th Avenue, S.
Lethbridge, Alberta T1J 0N9
403/327-5724

Minburn Vermilion Health Unit
Box 682
Vermilion, Alberta T0B 4M0
403/853-5270

BRITISH COLUMBIA

Planned Parenthood-Comox
Valley
Upper Island Health Unit
480 Cumberland Road
Courtenay, B.C. V9N 5N3
604/334-3141

Planned Parenthood-South Delta
Ladner Public Health Unit
4470-57th Street
Clarence Taylor Crescent
Delta, B.C. V4K 3W3
604/946-1221

Planned Parenthood-Cowichan
P.O. Box 54
Duncan, B.C. V9L 3X1
604/748-1511

Planned Parenthood-Langley
Central Fraser Valley Health Unit
22033 Fraser Highway
Langley, B.C. V3A 4H2
604/534-9221

Planned Parenthood-Nanaimo
149 Wallace Street
Nanaimo, B.C. V9R 5B2
604/752-9511

Planned Parenthood-New
Westminster
537 Carnarvon Street
New Westminster, B.C. V3L 1C2
604/521-5122

Planned Parenthood-Port Alberni
c/o Public Health Unit
4711 Elizabeth Street
Port Alberni, B.C. V9Y 6M1
604/724-7281

Planned Parenthood-Port
Coquitlam
2266 Wilson Avenue
Port Coquitlam, B.C. V3C 1Z5
604/941-3451

Planned Parenthood-Prince
  Rupert
Skeena Health Unit
333-5th Street
Prince Rupert, B.C. V8J 3P8

Planned Parenthood-Surrey/
  White Rock/Delta
Box 163; 1549 Johnston Road
Surrey, B.C. V4B 3Z6
604/531-5508

Planned Parenthood-Whalley
Whalley Public Health Unit
13674 Grosvenor Road
Surrey, B.C. V3R 5E2
604/581-6141

Family Service of Greater
  Vancouver
1616 West Seventh Avenue
Vancouver, B.C. V6J 1S5
604/731-4951

Planned Parenthood Assn. of
  B.C.
96 East Broadway, Suite 101
Vancouver, B.C. V5T 1V6
604/872-8737

Planned Parenthood-North
  Vancouver
4339 Ruth Crescent
Vancouver, B.C. V7K 2N1
604/872-0032

Planned Parenthood-Vancouver
#206-2525 Pine Street
Vancouver, B.C. V6J 3E8
604/736-8788

Planned Parenthood-Vernon
3105B-31st Avenue
Vernon, B.C. V1T 2G9
604/545-2034

Planned Parenthood-Victoria
c/o Metropolitan Board of
  Health
1947 Cook Street
Victoria, B.C. V8T 3P7
604/477-6911

MANITOBA

Planned Parenthood Manitoba,
  Inc.
112-6th Street
Brandon, Manitoba R7A 3N2
204/727-0417

Family Services of Winnipeg
287 Broadway Avenue
Winnipeg, Manitoba R3C 0R9
204/947-1401

Planned Parenthood Manitoba
1000-259 Portage
Winnipeg, Manitoba R3B 2A9
204/943-6489

**NEW BRUNSWICK/
NOUVEAU BRUNSWICK**

L'Association de la Planification
  des naissances
C.P. 733
Edmundston, Nouveau
  Brunswick E3V 3S1
506/735-4725

Northern Carleton Family
   Planning Association
P.O. Box 120
Florenceville, New Brunswick
   E0J 1K0
506/392-5296

Planned Parenthood Federation
749 Charlotte Street
Fredericton, New Brunswick
E3B 1M6
506/454-6333

Planned Parenthood New
   Brunswick, Inc.
Victoria Health Centre
43 rue Brunswick Street
Fredericton, New Brunswick
E3B 1G5
506/454-1808

L'Association de la Planification
   Familiale de Kedgwick-St-
   Quentin
C.P. 207
Kedgwick, Nouveau Brunswick
   E0K 1C0
506/284-2821

Planned Parenthood Moncton
25½ Grandview Drive
Moncton, New Brunswick
E1E 3J9
506/854-4952

L'Association de la Planification
   des naissances de Bathurst
C.P. 178
Petit-Rocher
Nouveau Brunswick E0B 2E0
506/546-9293

Planned Parenthood Sackville
P.O. Box 1195
Sackville, New Brunswick
E0A 3C0
506/536-1342

Saint John Planned Parenthood
   Assoc.
62 Carmarthen Street
Saint John, New Brunswick
E2L 2N5
506/693-8454

**NEWFOUNDLAND/
TERRE-NEUVE**

Planned Parenthood
   Newfoundland/Labrador
Fort William Building
21 Factory Lane
St. John's, Newfoundland
A1C 3J8
709/753-7333

**NORTHWEST TERRITORIES/
TERRITOIRES DU
   NORD-OUEST**

Planned Parenthood N.W.T.
P.O. Box 1680
Yellowknife, N.W.T. X0E 1H0
403/873-6112

**NOVA SCOTIA/
NOUVELLE-ECOSSE**

Planned Parenthood Association
   of Halifax, Dartmouth and
   Halifax Co.
5239 Young Street
Halifax, Nova Scotia B3K 5L4
902/455-9656

Planned Parenthood Association
 of Nova Scotia
1815 Hollis Street
Halifax, Nova Scotia B3J 1W3
902/423-2090

Family Planning Resource Team
Sydney City Hospital
Urquhart Hall
Whitney Avenue
Sydney, Nova Scotia B1P 2H8
902/539-5158

The Well Woman Clinic
60 Vancouver Street
Yarmouth, Nova Scotia B5A 2P5
902/742-8451

ONTARIO

Planned Parenthood Guelph
177 Norfolk Street
Guelph, Ontario N1H 4K1
519-836-7430

Family Services of Hamilton-
 Wentworth
First Place
350 King Street East
Suite 201
Hamilton, Ontario L8N 3Y3
416/523-5640

Planned Parenthood Society of
 Hamilton
4 Catherine Street North
Hamilton, Ontario L8R 1H8
416/528-3009

Adolescent Clinic
c/o C.O.P.C.
Stuart Street
Kingston General Hospital
Kingston, Ontario K7L 2V7
613/547-2121

Planned Parenthood Waterloo
 Region
119 King Street West
Suite 1
Kitchner, Ontario N2G 1A7
519/743-3842

Adolescent Clinic
Box 34
Moose Factory General Hospital
Moose Factory, Ontario
P0L 1W0
705/658-4544

Family Planning Center
269 Main Street West
Sibbitt Centre
North Bay, Ontario P1B 2T8
705/472-6515

Health Promotion Directorate
 Resource Center
Health and Welfare Canada
Jeanne Mance Building
Tunney's Pasture
Ottawa, Ontario K1A 1B4
613/996-1545

Planned Parenthood Federation
 of Canada
15 Slater Street
Suite 200
Ottawa, Ontario K1P 5H3
613/722-3484

Planned Parenthood Ottawa, Inc.
1355 Bank Street
Suite 206
Ottawa, Ontario K1H 8K7
613/523-8303 or 523-8204

Planned Parenthood Association
of Niagara
3 King Street
Suite 5
St. Catharines, Ontario L2R 3G8
416/688-3817

Adolescent Clinic
Hospital for Sick Children
Toronto, Ontario M5G 1X8
416/597-1500

Family Planning Services
Department of Public Health
City of Toronto
37 Spadina Road
Toronto, Ontario M5R 2S9
416/961-8459
*HOTLINE: 416/367-7442

Family Service Association of
Metropolitan Toronto
22 Wellesley Street East
Toronto, Ontario M4Y 1G3
416/922-3126

Ontario Ministry of Health
Family Health Unit
15 Overlea Boulevard
Toronto, Ontario M4H 1A9
416/965-5055

Planned Parenthood of Toronto
58 Shaftesbury Avenue
Toronto, Ontario M4T 1A3
416/961-8290

Sex Information and Education
Council of Canada (SIECCAN)
423 Castlefield Avenue
Toronto, Ontario M5N 1L4
416/483-8805

Y.W.C.A.
80 Woodlawn Avenue East
Toronto, Ontario M4Y 1C1
416/961-8100

Planned Parenthood Ontario
P.O. Box 831
Waterloo, Ontario N2J 4C2
519/743-6461

I.O.D.E. Children's Centre
4001 Leslie Street
Willowdale, Ontario M2K 1E1
416/492-3836

Family Service Bureau of
Windsor
450 Victoria Avenue
Windsor, Ontario N9A 6T1
519/256-1831

**PRINCE EDWARD ISLAND/
ILE-DU-PRINCE-EDOUARD**

Planned Parenthood of P.E.I.
218 Kent Street
Charlottetown, P.E.I. C1A 4B6
902/892-8141

QUEBEC

Service de Gaspe pour la
planification des naissances
C.P. 206
Gaspe, Quebec G0C 1R0
418/368-1929

Association du planning des
naissances de l'Outaouais-Sud
C.P. 1305
Hull, Quebec J8X 3Y1
819/777-2856

Association du planning des
naissances du Saguenay-Lac
St.-Jean
C.P. 794
Jonquiere, Quebec G7X 2Y6
418/548-2106

Association pour le planning des
naissance pour la region-sud de
Montreal
a/s Centre Diocesain
740 Boulevard Ste. Foy
Longueil, Quebec J4J 1Z3
514/679-1100

Adolescent Unit
Allan Memorial Institute
1025 Pine Avenue West
Montreal, Quebec H3A 1A1
514/842-1231

Adolescent Unit
Montreal Children's Hospital
2300 Tupper Street
Montreal, Quebec H3H 1P3
514/937-8511

La Federation du Quebec pour le
planning des naissances
3826 rue St. Hubert
Montreal, Quebec H2L 4A5
514/842-9501

Montreal Planned Parenthood
Assn.
336 Sherbrooke Street, East
Montreal, Quebec H2X 1E6
514/844-3349

Ste.-Justine Hospital
3175 Cote Ste.-Catherine Road
Montreal, Quebec H3T 1C5
514/731-4931

Ville Marie Social Service Center
4018 St. Catherine Street, West
Montreal, Quebec H3Z 1P2
514/989-1885

Association de planning des
naissances du Bas du Fleuve
167 St. Louis
Rimouski, Quebec G5L 5R2
418/722-4797

Association regionale du Nord-
ouest pour le planning familial
C.P. 1051
Rouyn, Quebec J9X 5C8
819/764-4714

Association du planning familial
des Sept-iles
405 ave Brochu
Sept-iles, Quebec G4R 2W9
418/962-5562

Association de planification des
naissances de
Mauricie-Bois-Francs
2352-43e Rue
Shawinigan, Quebec G9N 5E8
819/539-3030

Association de l'Estrie pour la
planification des naissances
509 rue London
Sherbrooke, Quebec J1H 3M9
819/567-2427

Association pour la planification
des naissances de la region de
Quebec
180 rue Blouin
Ville Vanier, Quebec G1M 1E3
418/681-0285

SASKATCHEWAN

Battlefords Planned Parenthood
1-1064-101st Street
North Battleford, Saskatchewan
S9A 0Z3
306/445-6239

Catholic Family Service Society
1120-11th Avenue
Regina, Saskatchewan S4P 0G3
306/525-0521

Catholic Family Services
635 Main Street
Saskatoon, Saskatchewan
S7H 0J8
306/244-7773

Family Service Bureau
200-245 3rd Avenue, South
Saskatoon, Saskatchewan
S7K 1M4
306/244-0127

Planned Parenthood
Saskatchewan
#404-245 Third Avenue South
Saskatoon, Saskatchewan
S7K 1M4
306/664-2050

Planned Parenthood Saskatoon
Centre
530-10th Street East
Saskatoon, Saskatchewan
S7N 0E2
306/244-7989

YUKON

Yukon Planned Parenthood
207 Elliot Street
Whitehorse, Yukon Y1A 2A1
403/667-2970

The Salvation Army
Maternity Homes in Canada

Calgary Park Wood House
1340-8th Avenue, N.W.
Calgary, Alberta
403/284-2293

Vancouver Maywood Home
7250 Oak Street
Vancouver, British Columbia
604/266-6931

Winnipeg Lindenview Residence
250 Booth Drive
Winnipeg, Manitoba
204/889-8830

Halifax Bethany Home
980 Tower Road
Halifax, Nova Scotia
902/422-5900

Sydney Parkdale House
47 Byng Avenue
Sydney, Nova Scotia
902/562-5827

Hamilton Grace Haven
138 Herkimer Street
Hamilton, Ontario
416/522-7350

London Bethesda Centre
54 Riverview Avenue
London, Ontario
519/438-8371

Ottawa Bethany Home
1140 Wellington Street
Ottawa, Ontario
613/722-4737

Thunder Bay Florence Booth
   Home
497 N. Lillie Street
Thunder Bay, Ontario
807/623-0232

Toronto Bethany Home and Day
   Care
450 Pape Avenue
Toronto, Ontario
416/461-0217

Regina Grace Haven
2301-15th Avenue
Regina, Saskatchewan
306/352-1421

Saskatoon Bethany Home
802 Queen Street
Saskatoon, Saskatchewan
306/244-6758

BIBLIOGRAPHY

"Adolescent Pregnancy and Childbearing." Department of Health, Education, and Welfare, October, 1981.

"Adolescent Pregnancy and Childbearing—Growing Concerns for Americans." *Population Bulletin.* Population Reference Bureau, Inc., September 1976.

Bell, Ruth and others. *Changing Bodies, Changing Lives.* Random House, Inc., 1980.

Black, Pamela. "Abortion Affects Men, Too." *The New York Times Magazine.* March 28, 1982.

"Black and White, Unwed All Over." *Time* Magazine, November 9, 1981.

Butcher, Ruth L. and Robinson, Marion O. "The Unmarried Mother." Public Affairs Committee, 1959.

"Caring for Two." Planned Parenthood Federation of America, Inc., 1981.

Carson, Ruth. "So You Want to Adopt a Child." Public Affairs Committee, Inc., 1966.

Cheek, David. "Involving Adolescent Unmarried Fathers." *Office of Adolescent Pregnancy Programs Information Bulletin,* February, 1981.

"Considering What to Do." Planned Parenthood Federation of America, Inc., 1981.

Cowart, B.S., M.A., Eileen and Liston, Ed.D., Walter. "For the Young Mother-to-Be." Mead Johnson Laboratories, 1975.

"Deciding on Abortion." Planned Parenthood Federation of America, 1981.

Dickman, Irving R. "Teenage Pregnancy—What Can Be Done?" Public Affairs Committee, Inc. 1981.

"11 Million Teenagers—What Can Be Done About the Epidemic Adolescent Pregnancies in the United States." The Alan Guttmacher Institute, 1976.

"Expectant Mother's Guide." Gerber Products Company, 1974.

"For the Never Married Mother." Parents Without Partners, 1972.

Francke, Linda Bird. *The Ambivalence of Abortion.* Dell Publishing Company, Inc., 1978.

Garvis, Marlene and others. "Outreach Teaching." International Childbirth Education Association, 1979.

Ginott, Dr. Haim G. *Between Parent and Teenager.* Avon Books 1969.

Gordon, Ph.D., Sol. *You Would If You Loved Me.* Bantam Books, 1979.

Grow, Lucille J. *Early Childrearing by Young Mothers.* Child Welfare League of America, 1979.

Guttmacher, M.D., Alan F. *Pregnancy, Birth, and Family Planning.* The Viking Press, Inc., 1973.

Haitch, Richard. "Orphans of the Living—The Foster Care Crisis." Public Affairs Committee, 1968.

Hansen, Caryl. *Your Choice.* Avon Books, 1980.

Howard, Marion. "Comprehensive Community Programs for the Pregnant Teenager." *Clinical Obstetrics and Gynecology,* June, 1971.

Howard, Marion. *Only Human—Teenage Pregnancy and Parenthood.* Avon Books, 1975.

"How to Talk to Your Teenagers About Something Not Easy to Talk About." Planned Parenthood Federation of America, Inc., 1976.

Kelly, Gary F. *Learning About Sex—The Contemporary Guide for Young Adults.* Barrow's Educational Series, Inc., 1976.

Klein, Carole. *The Single Parent Experience.* Avon Books, 1973.

Leishman, Katie. "Teenage Mothers." *Ms. Magazine,* June 1980.

Leo, John. "Single Parent, Double Trouble." *Time* Magazine, January 4, 1982.

Lieberman, M.D., E. James and Peck, Ellen. *Sex and Birth Control.* Thomas Y. Crowell, 1973.

Lindsay, Jeanne Warren. *Pregnant Too Soon—Adoption Is an Option.* Morning Glory Press, 1980.

MacLachlan, Edith A. and Cole, Elma Phillipson. "The Salvation Army Education for Parenthood Program." *Children Today Magazine,* May-June, 1978.

"Maternal Nutrition and the Course of Pregnancy." United States Department of Health, Education, and Welfare, 1970.

McCoy, Kathy and Wibbelsman, M.D., Charles. *The Teenage Body Book.* Pocket Books, 1978.

Meezan, William; and others. *Adoption Without Agencies.* Child Welfare League of America, 1978.

Mitchell, Joyce Slayton. *Other Choices for Becoming a Woman.* Dell Publishing Company, Inc., 1975.

Nye, F. Ivan. "School-Age Parenthood." Washington State University Cooperative Extension Service, 1976.

Oettinger, Katherine B. *Not My Daughter—Facing Up to Adolescent Pregnancy.* Prentice-Hall, Inc., 1979.

Ogg, Elizabeth. "Unmarried Teenagers and Their Children." Public Affairs Committee, 1976.

Pomeroy, Ph.D., Wardell B. *Girls and Sex.* Dell Publishing Company, Inc., 1981.

"Prenatal Care." United States Department of Health, Education, and Welfare, 1973.

Sarrel, M.S.W., Lorna J. and Sarrel, M.D. Philip M. *Sexual Unfolding— Sexual Development and Sex Therapies in Late Adolescence.* Little, Brown and Company, 1979.

Schwartz, M.D., June V. and Botts, R.N., Emma R. "The Very New Baby: The First Days of Life." Public Affairs Committee, Inc. 1977.

"Teenage Pregnancy." *International Childbirth Education Association Newsletter for Teachers,* February, 1980.

"Teenager Pregnancy: The Problem that Hasn't Gone Away." Alan Guttmacher Institute, 1981.

"Teensex—It's OK to Say No Way." Planned Parenthood Federation of America, Inc., 1979.

Terkelsen, Helen E. "I'm Going to Have a Baby and I'm Not Married." Fortress Press, 1968.

Tizard, Barbara. *Adoption: A Second Chance.* The Free Press, 1977.

Tod, Linda. "Labor and Birth." International Childbirth Education, 1981.

"What's Happening Now." Fulton-Dekalb Hospital Authority, 1980.

"What Teens Want to Know but Don't Know How to Ask." Planned Parenthood Federation of America, Inc., 1976.

Whelan, Sc.D., Dr. Elizabeth M. *A Baby?... Maybe.* The Bobbs-Merrill Company, Inc., 1980.

Zitner, Rosalind and Miller, Shelby Hayden. "Our Youngest Parents." Child Welfare League of America, 1980.

Index

Jeannine Masterson Michael, M.S.W., C.S.W., has been practicing in the field of family planning and reproductive health since 1973. She specializes in decision-making counseling with adolescents who are in a state of crisis due to unplanned pregnancy. Ms. Michael is the director of counseling at Eastern Women's Center, a gynecological health care facility in New York City, and is also in private practice. She lectures frequently on the psychological aspects of unwanted pregnancy and conducts training workshops for counselors in this field. Ms. Michael and her family live in New Jersey.

Reni L. Witt is a free-lance writer who specializes in books about human and family relationships. Her work also includes creating original screenplays for television as well as developing and editing books. She lives with her husband in Westchester County, New York.